The
Kolel in
America

Herbert W. Bomzer

The Kolel in America

SHENGOLD PUBLISHERS, INC.

New York City

ISBN 0-88400-118-9
Library of Congress Catalog Card Number: 85-63012
Copyright © 1985 by Herbert W. Bomzer

Published by Shengold Publishers, Inc.
23 W. 45th St., New York, N.Y. 10036

Printed in the United States of America

Contents

Acknowledgments

Gratitude is a sign of recognition that achievement of a goal is seldom self-made, but is due to the help, advice, cooperation, guidance, and friendship of many.

I am eternally grateful to the Almighty, Who granted me the privilege of studying with the great luminaries of our time. Rav Moshe Aharon Poleyeff, Z"L, Rav Aharon Kotler, Z"L, Rav Nissen Telushkin, Z"L, Rav Joseph Dov Soloveitchik, Shlita, and Rav Moshe Feinstein, Shlita, my mentors and leaders of *klal yisrael*, have influenced and guided my life. I pay special tribute to the Rebbe of Lubavitch, HaAdmor Rav Menachem Mendel Schneerson, Shlita.

I am indebted to Yeshiva University for my education and for the opportunity to teach Torah to two generations of young men and women. The President, Rabbi Dr. Norman Lamm, and his administrators urged and enabled me to undertake and complete this study.

I am grateful to Dr. Menachem M. Brayer, Chairman of my Sponsoring Committee, for his invaluable encouragement, teachings, and expertise. I thank Dr. Norman Bronznick for his talented counsel, and Dr. Yitzchak S. Handel for his personal interest and assistance.

I thank the *Roshei Yeshivah*, the administrators, the *Roshei Kolel*, the *kolel* fellows, their wives, the rabbis and all who generously gave of their time to provide the data needed for this study.

I gratefully acknowledge the help of Goldie Wachsman, a most conscientious editor, and of Moshe Sheinbaum, President of Shengold Publishers; their professional advice proved invaluable.

I owe a debt of thanks to the officers and members of my congregation, Young Israel of Ocean Parkway, where I have been privileged to serve as Spiritual Leader for over thirty years. Their support and respect have enabled me to devote the time and energy to this study.

My gratitude is expressed to Mr. and Mrs. Ulo Barad, Mr. and Mrs. Peter Benenfeld, Mr. and Mrs. Joseph Dunietz and the Executive Board of Young Israel of Ocean Parkway for their help in publishing this book.

My loving thanks go to my wonderful family: to Rabbi Moshe and Rochel, Ettie and Paul, Gedaliah and Renee, Zipporah and Joshua, Esther and Menachem, and Suri. Their goodness helped so much, particularly in difficult moments. One could not ask for better children.

Aharon aharon haviv, finally, I am forever indebted to my wife, Leona. Her patience, encouraging support, hard work, and continuous love made possible the completion of this research. I dedicate this work to her, in loving appreciation.

Tevet, 5746   H.W.B
January, 1986

Introduction

Jewish religious education in the United States from early childhood through advanced professional training has been the subject of numerous studies.[1] Academic and popular analyses and a variety of fictional accounts have portrayed the history, curricula, administrative concerns, and educational methodology of day schools, traditional *yeshivot* (sing. *yeshivah*), afternoon and Sunday schools, advanced Jewish study, and rabbinical training programs. Some have praised their accomplishments, others have criticized their practices, while still others have attempted to assess their future and their impact upon the quality of Jewish life in America.

The one unit of Jewish education in America that has been largely neglected in such analyses is the *kolel* (pl. *kolelim*). Serving as the postgraduate division of many larger *yeshivot*, and occasionally a free-standing institution in its own right, it was estimated that by 1981 some sixty *kolelim* existed in the United States.[2] The phenomenon represents both an extention of a mode of study fairly well known in nineteenth-century Europe and a novel approach to Jewish education in the United States. Nevertheless, little has been done to describe the structure, program, faculty, students, or social environment of the *kolel*. Nor has a serious attempt been made to consider the significance of the *kolel* for Jewish education in general.

Despite this scholarly neglect, it is clear that the *kolel* is a growing facet of Jewish cultural life. Though it first appeared on the American scene no more than forty years ago, its growth both in terms of the number of institutions and the number of students has been impressive. In addition, alumni of many *kolelim* are now assuming positions of influence within Jewish educational and communal organizations, extending the impact of the *kolel* and increasing the number of potential students. It was both the paucity of existing literature and the author's conviction that the *kolel* has become, and will continue to be, an important force in Jewish education and religious life that motivated the present study.

Within this context, it is the writer's intention to provide a history of the transplantation of the *kolel* to American soil, to describe its curriculum, the kind of student it attracts, and its general impact upon the Jewish community locally and nationally. A cross section of institutions will be presented individually, in the hope of defining their goals and objectives, their common features, and their differences. These will be detailed in terms of structure, program, physical environment, faculty, alumni, etc. Both the strengths and shortcomings of the *kolel* will be included so that a balanced and objective picture of this institution may emerge.

Kolel Typology

Choosing the subjects of such a study has not been easy. The various institutions differ along several lines, and an effort was made to include subjects that would be representative of the full cross section. Some *kolelim* are large and of long standing, others are small and of recent vintage. Some are the natural successors to European institutions, whereas others trace their beginnings to these shores. Some are affiliated with a broader community or a lower-division school, and others are largely independent.

In addition to certain structural differences, the institutions diverge in their focus and curriculum. Some stand in the Lithuanian tradition of encyclopedic erudition and the study of *musar* (ethics), and others are born of the *hasidic* tradition, attaching themselves to a particular religious leader and shaping their program of study to the needs of their community. Most discourage secular education, although a few facilitate or even require a university degree. Clearly, any attempt to formulate a typology within which representative institutions could be chosen would be quite difficult, fraught with qualitative overlap, and often lacking in rigor.

Nevertheless four categories, based on the history of the institution, its academic format, and empirical observation, have been established in order to aid in the selection and evaluation of subjects. These are the Lithuanian, the *hasidic*, the "new" *kolel*, and the community *kolel*. Each will be examined in its turn, and a listing of the members of each typology follows below.

The Lithuanian *kolel* is generally a direct descendant of an institution established in Lithuania prior to World War II or one whose founder was a prestigious graduate of such a school. It is uniformly the graduate division of a larger *yeshivah* but not specifically affiliated with a particular community or segment of Jewish life. Students at such a *kolel* often constitute a self-contained community whose leader is the *rosh yeshivah*, or dean and senior professor of the school. With certain limited and recent exceptions, these *kolelim* have not aggressively pursued outreach programs aimed at the broader Jewish community or at those on the fringes of Jewish life.

Academically, these institutions focus almost exclusively upon the study of Talmud. Some appear more concerned with *beki'ut*, the broad and far-reaching familiarity with Talmudic text and interpretation. Others emphasize *harifut*, the in-depth analysis of fewer texts, with an eye towards sharpening the student's insight into the basic principles of Talmudic study. Of course, neither orientation is completely exclusive of the other.[3]

Another curricular element characteristic of this group of *kolelim* is the concern with the study of *musar*, a particular brand of Jewish ethics whose academic methodology includes the study of specially chosen classical texts, introspection, and a regimen for personal self-improvement. Traditionally, the *yeshivah* would provide a regularly scheduled talk known as a *musar shmu'es*, delivered by the *mashgi'ah*. In most instances, the *mashgi'ah* held a place of great prestige within the institution, second only to the *rosh yeshivah* himself.

Observation suggests, however, that *musar* is far less important to the American *kolel*, even within the Lithuanian type of schools. Some offer only sporadic sessions for its study; most are voluntary and few are well attended. In many cases the individual student may choose to substitute the study of *musar* with some other topic more attuned to his personal or social needs. In certain cases, the study of *hasidic* thought is an acceptable alternative.

The second group of institutions is the *hasidic kolelim*. These are schools affiliated with a particular *hasidic* community and the various educational and social agencies that fall under its control. The *kolel*, the *yeshivah*, and the entire community that sponsors the *kolel* owe allegiance to a *hasidic* leader known as the *rebbe*, or grand rabbi. Generally, he is the scion of a dynasty of leaders first established in eighteenth- or nineteenth-century Europe.

Traditionally, Torah study in *hasidic* communities was far less formal than among their Lithuanian counterparts. The *yeshivah* was largely oriented towards primary education, and adult study was relegated to after-hours and holidays. Rather than create a formal institution for higher education, *hasidim* would study in the *rebbe*'s synagogue, known as a *klaus* in Galicia, or the *shtibl* in Poland.

Thus, in the *hasidic* milieu, there was no *kolel* in the formal sense. Advanced students spent much of their time at the synagogue, working at their own pace, only informally supervised, and subject to very little curricular structure. The core of study was Talmud and the contemporary decisions and interpretations of Jewish law, with an emphasis on practical concerns. The purpose was less to create scholars in the academic sense than to produce those who could apply their study to the practical needs of the community and the problems that might arise therefrom.[4]

As a result, the *kolel* is a relative newcomer to *hasidic* life. Introduced in postwar America, it has not fully taken hold among the faithful, and its legitimacy has had to be defended in the effort to mobilize social and financial support for its program. As a result, *hasidic kolelim* differ from those affiliated with Lithuanian *yeshivot* in terms of curriculum, structure, and wider communal support—an assertion that is documented in the pages that follow.

A third category of *kolelim* has been titled the "new" *kolelim* because of the lack of a common denominator among them. Each school in this category might have been placed in either the Lithuanian or *hasidic* category. However, because these institutions differ significantly from both categories in terms of entrance standards, requirements, curricular orientation, or goals, a third category had to be assigned for these schools. The three chosen to represent the new *kolelim* would likely be uncomfortable in each other's company because of fundamental differences among them, but they have at least one thing in common: each represents a new experimentation within the concept of the *kolel*.

Finally, a fourth type of *kolel*, the community *kolel*, is discussed. This phenomenon is a very recent addition to the world of American Jewish education and has not received much scholarly attention. The community *kolel* is an institution that attempts to fulfill two goals simultaneously. In the first instance, its hope is to remain loyal to the classic definition of the *kolel* by Lithuanian standards. It aspires to be a place of profound Torah study for married students and to produce scholars and intellectuals who will serve the faculties of other programs of higher learning. Indeed, virtually all such schools maintain institutional, educational, and personal links with larger, better established, and traditional *yeshivot* or *kolelim*, at which most of their faculty were trained.

Second, the community *kolel* is distinguished by its dual commitment to religious studies and to programs of outreach and community service. These institutions do not isolate themselves, nor do they view normal contact with the outside negatively. Rather, the community *kolel* attempts to forge links with its neighbors through programs of adult education, counseling, religious services and rituals, and youth activities. By the same token, it depends in large measure upon these neighbors for its financial support.

The first community *kolel* in North America was founded in Toronto in 1970. Since then, several such *kolelim* have been established in major cities throughout the United States, including Denver, St. Louis, Philadelphia, and Los Angeles. After a lengthy discussion with R. Dov Lesser of Torah U'mesorah, the National Association of Jewish Day Schools, it was decided that the study of several such institutions would be redundant, and only two were therefore chosen as representative of all community *kolelim*, since all follow the same goals and methods with essentially similar populations.[5]

Given this typology, the following sample of *kolelim* was chosen, and this work is limited to the analysis of the history, development, and current status of these institutions.

GROUP I—THE LITHUANIAN KOLELIM
1. Beth Medrash Govoha,[6] The Rabbi Aaron Kotler Institute for Advanced Learning of Lakewood, New Jersey.
2. Mirrer Yeshiva Central Institute, Brooklyn, New York.
3. Ner Israel Rabbinical College, Baltimore, Maryland.
4. Gur Aryeh Institute for Advanced Jewish Scholarship, Mesivta Chaim Berlin, Brooklyn, New York.
5. Kolel Ner David of Yeshivat Rabbi Israel Meir Hakohen, Rabbinical Seminary of America, Queens, New York.

GROUP II—THE HASIDIC KOLELIM
1. Central Yeshiva Tomchei Tmimin-Lubavitch, Brooklyn, New York.
2. Rabbinical College Bobover Yeshiva, Brooklyn, New York.
3. Kolel of Mesivta Zanz, Union City, New Jersey.
4. Kolel Avreikhim of Gur, Brooklyn, New York.

GROUP III—THE NEW KOLELIM
1. Yeshiva University, New York, New York.
2. Kolel Mechon Hahoyroa, Monsey, New York.
3. Kollel Horabonim, Monsey, New York.

GROUP IV—THE COMMUNITY KOLEL
1. Kollel Bais Avrohom of Los Angeles, California.
2. Kolel Yeshiva Gedolah Zichron Moshe, Fallsburg, New York.

Methodology

On-site visits of each institution were arranged and interviews conducted with its faculty, administration, students and their families, and
alumni. Interviews were uniformly conducted after questionnaires had
been answered by those interviewed (see Appendix). A total of 43 *roshei
yeshivah* (senior faculty) and administrators were interviewed, along with
65 students, 30 alumni, 20 local rabbis, 20 local lay leaders, 18 wives of
kolel students, and 10 parents. In addition, the author spent several hours
in study at each institution, observing social and educational patterns, student-faculty relations, classroom technique, and independent research. In
some instances, he was also invited to deliver lectures to *kolel* students
and observe their preparation and responsiveness.

The research was carried out during the academic years 1981–83. Interviews were candid and confidential, and the subjects were most coopera-
tive. In addition there was access to most school literature and to the self-
study documents published under the direction of the Association of Advanced Rabbinical and Talmudic Schools (AARTS), a voluntary organization that accredits graduate programs in rabbinic studies.[7]

The Plan of Study

Part One begins with a historical survey of the growth of the *kolel* as an
educational form in nineteenth-century Europe and twentieth-century
America. Part Two devotes one unit to each of the fourteen institutions
studied. Thus, the *kolel* itself is the unit of analysis.

Within each unit, the *kolel* is described in terms of its history, the great
scholars whose tutelage it follows, and its educational philosophy and
goals. Consideration is also given to the curriculum, educational methods,
and the training and recruitment of faculty and students.

An analysis of the student body is also presented; entrance standards,
financial aid, living arrangements, student families, and relations with
alumni are discussed. The result is a comprehensive portrait of fourteen
individual *kolelim*, offered from several perspectives.

Part Three is comparative analysis of the data culled. Here an attempt is
made to delineate similarities and differences between the institutions and
to suggest what these may indicate. The emphasis here is not upon simple
description, but rather upon an explanation of these phenomena within the
context of the given institution's history, goals, leadership, and other factors. Where appropriate, quantitative data are presented and analyzed in

order to document these conclusions, although the thrust of the presentation is qualitative. The data provided by the institutions have been judged by the author on the basis of personal observation. Part Four contains the author's impressions and conclusions.

Related Literature

To date, discussions of the *kolel* in the literature have been limited to descriptions of a few large institutions and to popular reflections on the topic. The paucity of scholarly literature offering a comprehensive treatment of the *kolel* in America was all the more apparent following the author's review of the catalogues at the libraries of Yeshiva University, the Jewish Theological Seminary, and the Hebrew Union College.[8] What has been written is not impressive.

Nisson Wolpin and Mendel Rokeach outline the history of the establishment of major *kolelim* in the United States.[9] Both of their magazine articles are rather restrictive and selective in treatment, yet do succeed in a popular way to describe the early development of the *kolelim* and the difficulties related to their growth. Of particular interest are Wolpin's descriptions of the growing interrelationship between the *kolel* and the general Jewish community. Continuing education programs, referral services, religious and cultural activities, and the community work of alumni are indicative of such a trend. In addition, those for whom access to Jewish life is limited and difficult are served by the creation of "pilot community *kolelim*" and annexes modeled after the parent institution.

In this regard, both Rokeach in 1963 and Wolpin in 1979 conclude that Torah has "come of age" in America. But these articles are indicative of the paucity of material on the subject. They deal with only a handful of *kolelim*, completely omitting mention of such institutions as Yeshiva University, Lubavitch, and a host of other *hasidic kolelim*.

Alvin I. Schiff, in his analysis of American Jewish education, offers a brief discussion of the *kolel* as an educational form.[10] He describes the structure of these institutions briefly, emphasizing the importance of self-motivation and material sacrifice among the students and their genuine desire to devote themselves to Torah study. It is his contention that the majority of those graduating from such programs "enter the teaching profession as Talmud instructors in the various *yeshivot* and *mesivtot* [Jewish parochial schools]." In this sense, he concludes that the *kolel* has had an influence, albeit indirect, upon the quality of Jewish education generally. However an evaluation of his conclusions in the light of contemporary circumstances shows that the majority do not enter these fields because the job market is limited.

William Helmreich, in his study of the "world of the *yeshivah*," devotes little space to the *kolel* or the contribution it might make to the quality of Jewish education in America.[11] His few passing comments are rather critical. It is his contention that study in the *kolel* is more a matter of status in many circles and has lost much of its pristine quality. He also suggests that the *kolel* is likely to lose support in the coming generation as its financial backers dwindle and are not replaced by alumni willing (or able) to fund a new generation of budding scholars.

Although far more superficial, David Singer is harshly critical of the educational method and pedagogic style of the individual *kolelim* he describes.[12] It is his belief that there is little accountability or discipline among students, and faculty members maintain little contact with their charges. He also raises questions about the caliber of students admitted to these institutions and the gap between the stated goals of a *kolel* and its actual accomplishments. These criticisms are discussed in the ensuing chapters.

Sidney Lewitter's analysis of the Beth Medrash Govoha of Lakewood, New Jersey, serves as an interesting case study both for its content and its methods.[13] However, as with all case studies, its value is limited since it is difficult to draw conclusions beyond the time and location of his work. For example, it is his contention that the inclusion of *musar* in the curriculum of the institution contributes handily to its success. Indeed, he urges all similar programs to adopt this element. Nevertheless, as will be demonstrated, the present research suggests that because of the composition of the student body at the Beth Medrash Govoha, the influence of *musar* has waned.

Finally, the monumental study of higher Jewish education in Europe, edited by Samuel Mirsky, serves as an excellent source of background material.[14] Its account of the various *yeshivot*, their early development, the personalities that shaped their programs, and their ultimate, often tragic decline, is an invaluable aid to understanding the transplantation of these institutions and their offshoots to these shores. Of course, this work is limited to pre-World War Europe and is of primarily historical value.

Despite its rather limited treatment in the literature, the *kolel* has much to offer American Jewry in several respects: it can set standards for primary and secondary education by training teachers and spiritual leaders; it can and does prepare learned laymen; and it serves as a center of religious and moral scholarhip and as a model for traditional values. It is the author's hope that the study of the modern *kolel* will be a useful contribution to Jewish educational literature and to the future implementation of curriculum in Jewish religious schools.

PART ONE
The Kolel in America

ROOTS AND DEVELOPMENT

Undoubtedly, the most important single responsibility incumbent upon the practicing Jew is the study of Torah.[1] This encompasses not only the Bible but the accumulated sum of rabbinic and classical Jewish literature, developed over a long period of time. Thus, "Torah" has become a generic term denoting a corpus of religious Jewish texts and sources.

For the Jew, the study of Torah is far more than a purely intellectual pursuit. In its essence, it may be considered a form of worship. Thus, the rabbis equate the scholar, immersing himself in intricacies of the Law, with one who performs the service in the ancient Temple.[2]

From the earliest times, Jews undertook this study within a formal academy known as a *yeshivah*. The rabbis were quite harsh in their judgment of any large Jewish settlements that neglected to establish *yeshivot* in their midst.[3] With the destruction of the Holy Temple by the Roman legions in 70 C.E., the Jewish people were further dispersed throughout the known world, and they transplanted this institution in the Diaspora. In the ensuing centuries, *yeshivot* were founded in Babylonia, North Africa, the Middle East, and later in Spain, Italy, France, and Eastern and Central Europe.

Initially the term *yeshivot* referred to an adult institution of higher learning, and it is only recently in America that the term has been applied to the elementary or secondary level. The Talmud records a debate regarding whether a man should marry prior to entering the halls of study or delay marriage until he had attained a reasonable level of scholarship. By all accounts, however, if he could be assured support, there was no reason to delay marriage.[4] Equally, the great medieval Jewish philosopher Maimonides (1135–1204) concludes:

> Even the pauper who is supported by charity or goes begging from door to door, and the man who has a wife and children to support, must set aside fixed periods by day and night for the study of Torah.[5]

It appears that full-time Torah study for those already married was prevalent in the early middle ages. They were supported by communities because they had no independent sources of income. Apparently, dependence on community support was not an isolated phenomenon, for it aroused the chagrin of Maimonides, codifier of Jewish law, who wrote:

> One who makes up his mind to study Torah and not work, and be supported by charity [funds], profanes the name of God, brings the Torah into contempt, extinguishes the light of religion, brings evil upon himself and deprives himself of life hereafter, for it is forbidden to derive any temporal advantage from the words of the Torah.[6]

Nevertheless, in more modern times, this form of study took hold among Jews of Lithuania. In 1803, R. Hayyim of Volozhin, a student of the rabbinic leader R. Elijah of Vilna, undertook the establishment of a major institution of higher Jewish learning in his own town. Funded by local residents, it allowed married students to continue their education unencumbered by the needs of the marketplace. He hoped to support an elite group of students in a respectable manner and with the esteem he felt they deserved. Such an institution was later to be called a *kolel*.[7]

Literally meaning a collection or collegium, the term *kolel* initially referred to a group of Ashkenazic Jewish settlers in nineteenth-century Palestine who stemmed from the same region in Europe. Financial support for these settlers, known as *halukkah*, was collected and apportioned according to place of origin. These groups were known as *kolelim* (gatherings or communities) as early as the 1830s. The term gained currency among European Jews and was soon applied to any group or community engaged in the performance of a vital religious task worthy of popular economic support.[8]

The first application of the term to an institution of higher Jewish learning for newly married men may have been made by R. Israel Lipkin of Salant (1810–1883).[9] In 1878 he established the Kolel Perushim, an institution for those who would separate themselves for purposes of study. His intention may have been to capitalize upon the title and thereby imply that the study of Torah was an equally vital responsibility, requiring total concentration and deserving of community approbation and financial support.

The institution gave rise to the more contemporary meaning of the term *kolel* as a gathering or fellowship of scholars whose sole and prime purpose is *"Torah lishmah,"* the study of Torah for its own sake. Aside from the provision of basic financial support, there was to be no material profit or professional pursuit gained from the study, though it was assumed that some rabbinical or educational post might be available for the graduate. Even these occupations were to be accepted only as an extension of *"Torah lishmah."*

The first *kolelim* were established in the United States in 1943. One such *kolel*, the Beth Medrash Govoha of Lakewood, New Jersey, was founded by R. Aaron Kotler. An internationally renowned Talmudic scholar, R. Kotler immigrated to the United States in 1941 as a result of special asylum privileges granted by President Roosevelt to a select group of European scholars. R. Kotler had previously served as director of the Yeshivah of Kletsk and was well known for his forceful leadership and concern for Jewish education throughout the world.[10]

The second *kolel*, Beth Medrash Elyon of Monsey, New York, was an extension of an already existing *yeshivah*, the Mesivta Torah Vodaath of Brooklyn. Founded largely as a result of the efforts of R. Shraga Feivel Mendlowitz, Principal of Torah Vodaath, it was originally intended to serve as a teacher's seminary, preparing young men for careers in primary and secondary Jewish education. However, within the context of the German annihilation of European Jewry and at the urging of R. Kotler, R. Mendlowitz soon shifted the direction of the Beth Medrash Elyon toward an emphasis upon undistracted study and research for newly married Torah scholars.[11]

It should be noted that there were *yeshivot* established in America prior to the founding of these two *kolelim*. Many were graduating educators and ordaining rabbis who served the growing Jewish communities throughout the country. However, the *kolel* was a novel concept—generally foreign to the American values of practicality and pragmatic action. Its popularization awaited the arrival of refugees from Nazi terror, who helped introduce this peculiarly European mode of education. By the late 1970s, however, the idea had taken hold and many *kolelim* have since been developed in various parts of the United States.

The chapters that follow offer a detailed description of fourteen of these *kolelim*, followed by comparative analyses and evaluations. However, before discussing a particular *kolel*, a broad and introductory overview of the general structure, curriculum, methods, facilities, and student population of all *kolelim* is in order.

Kolel Structure

The typical American *kolel* is affiliated with a larger *yeshivah*, which may include programs extending from early childhood to postgraduate study. In the case of an institution established by a *hasidic* community, it may also be aligned with a variety of other communal or social welfare units. As a result, the physical facilities available are rarely the *kolel*'s alone, but are frequently shared and multifunctional.

Nevertheless, adequate privacy is generally provided. At a minimum, the *kolel* has the use of a *bet midrash* (study hall) and library with a rich collection of Talmudic and rabbinic volumes as well as contemporary works of commentary, responsa, homiletics, and the like. In *hasidic* institutions, these are supplemented by selections from the *hasidic* masters, notably the founders of the given dynasty. The *bet midrash* or library can also serve as a prayer hall, and frequently one large room fulfills all three needs.

Classrooms, dining facilities, administrative offices, and limited recreational facilities are usually shared with other units of the institution. Some *kolelim* are part of a campus where housing is provided for students and faculty. Others require that fellows and their families seek their own accommodations.

Application to the *kolel* is virtually uniform. Those who seek to join the *kolel* generally sit for an interview or oral examination with a member of the faculty or administration. There are rarely written examinations. Letters of reference from former instructors or rabbinic authorities are generally required, as well as some record of the student's accomplishments elsewhere.

These formalities are generally waived if the applicant is an alumnus of the institution's undergraduate division. In this case, he is well known to the administration and, in most cases, was invited to apply. References and examinations are no longer deemed necessary, and the applicant is accepted following a *pro forma* application. For many institutions, the bulk of applicants are graduates of the lower divisions, which results in self-contained, inbred isolationism.

Upon acceptance, the *kolel* fellow is granted a stipend by the institution, which varies substantially from *kolel* to *kolel*. In most cases, grants are calculated according to family size, and certain institutions have devised incentives linked to the quantity and quality of a student's progress. Work-study assignments, remedial work with younger students, adult education classes, and administrative work are often available to help supplement the fellow's income. Wives uniformly work outside the home, and parents are called upon—often formally by the institution—to support the student's endeavors.

In addition, *kolel* fellows are eligible for a variety of federal and state programs of aid for students and the needy. These include the Basic Educational Opportunity Grant, the Guaranteed Student Loan Program, the National Direct Student Loan, and the State Student Incentive Grant. *Kolel* students may also receive food stamps, Medicaid, and lower-income housing aid to supplement their income.

Program of Study

The *kolel* schedule is an intensive one. Most institutions operate eleven months each year, and several hold sessions year round, with time off only for Jewish holidays. Students attend five to six days each week; sessions are abbreviated on Fridays because of the approach of the Sabbath. The daily program begins with early prayers, generally about 7:00 A.M., and continues in one form or another until late into the night.

The daily schedule is divided into three uneven *sedarim* (sessions or units—sing. *seder*). The morning *seder* follows prayers and breakfast, and continues until early afternoon with time allotted for afternoon prayers. Students are then free for one to two hours and return for the second *seder* in the afternoon, generally about 3:00 P.M. The session continues until early evening, adjourning about 7:00 P.M. for dinner. The later *seder* follows and some students remain in the *bet midrash* until midnight.

It is not unusual, however, for married *kolel* students to fulfill their evening obligations with study at home—alone, with an unmarried fellow, or with a younger student in need of remedial aid. In addition, in some instances, fellows are required to lead adult classes or participate in alternative forms of outreach and community activities that supersede other evening activities.

As is typical of *yeshivah* study generally, *kolel* students prepare their assignments or undertake research in pairs, known as *hevrutot* (sing. *hevrutah*). Choice of a partner is usually voluntary, based upon friendship and personality. But it is not uncommon for the administration of the *kolel* to make individual changes in *hevrutot* if it is felt that one or both partners might profit intellectually or emotionally from such a change.

While study in pairs is a virtually universal phenomenon among *kolelim,* many have also employed a system of *haburot,* or group seminars (sing. *haburah*). These groups consist of several *hevrutot* meeting regularly both for purposes of preparation and review. Unique within the *haburah* is the requirement that each member present an original piece of research or lead group discussions on a rotating basis. This is known as "saying the *haburah*." Each member is free to evaluate the thesis being presented, and the discussion is both erudite and lively.

In some of the *kolelim* a senior fellow might be appointed *rosh haburah*, or seminar leader. It is his responsibility to organize and supervise the presentation of materials before the *haburah* as well as to lead discussions himself on a regular basis. As with the *hevrutot*, membership in a *haburah* is generally a voluntary affair, although it is far more common for assignments to be made by the administration or for transfers to be suggested.

As noted above, the *kolel* is frequently part of a larger *yeshivah,* and physical facilities as well as administrative or ancillary services are commonly shared. To a lesser extent, this is true of the faculty as well. The *rosh yeshivah* supervises the activities of the entire institution and may spend some of his time instructing the *kolel* groups individually or as a part of a broader lecture program to which other units of the institution are invited as well. Depending upon his personality, he may also forge personal relationships with the *kolel* fellows, inviting them to his home, providing personal, vocational, and family counseling, and serving generally as an intellectual and social model.

In *hasidic kolelim*, i.e., institutions linked to and supported by a *hasidic* community, the *rebbe* is also the *rosh yeshivah*. However, his communal and social commitments often make it difficult for him to maintain the same level of personal contact with *kolel* students, who represent a tiny minority of his flock. For them he will frequently be a distant figure whose views are interpreted indirectly or from afar. Nevertheless, *hasidic kolel* students and their families exhibit enormous loyalty toward the *rebbe* and his community, and speak of him in the most personal and intimate terms.

Aside from the *rosh yeshivah*, most *kolelim* will have faculty members assigned directly to their students and appointed by the *rosh yeshivah*. The *rosh hakolel*, or *kolel* director, is responsible for setting the curriculum, presenting regular lectures known as *shi'urim* (sing. *shi'ur*), and supervising independent study and research. He is generally a graduate of the *yeshivah* and *kolel* himself and may be an older contemporary of present *kolel* fellows.

Finally, the typical *kolel* faculty also includes a *mashgi'ah*, a supervisor and counselor. It is his responsibility to monitor attendance and punctuality, help with *hevrutah* and *haburah* assignments, informally oversee student progress, and generally relieve administrative or logistical difficulties that might retard study. He is also available for personal or career counseling and will often present a series of talks dealing with *musar*. The *mashigi'ah* is also frequently a graduate of the *yeshivah* and not much older than the fellows he supervises. In some cases he may be assigned to the *kolel* as part of his general duties within the *yeshivah*.

It is by no means easy to generalize about the curricula of the American *kolel*. Many of the older and larger institutions maintain a core of study that is fairly standard, although even among these, there are important variations. Other, less traditional institutions have moved into specialized areas of study almost to the exclusion of this core. Finally, some include students in determining curricula, others respond to perceived external needs, and still others follow prescriptions from above.

However, the following generalizations can be made. The primary text of study in almost all *kolelim* is the Talmud. This is supplemented by the study of the standard commentaries on the Talmud and the principal codes, and by the occasional study of ethical and homiletical works. In *kolelim* sponsored by *hasidic yeshivot*, *hasidic* works are studied as well.

The larger and more traditional *kolelim* frequently follow a rotation of seven to ten Talmudic tractates studied by the *yeshivah* generally, though these are not necessarily uniform from institution to institution. Sensing the narrow focus in such curricula, certain institutions have undertaken the study of the entire Talmud; marital, domestic, and civil law; educational methodology; and practical rabbinics. Some have included communal work, adult study, or outreach programs, and others encourage or even require university education.

Students

Although the curricula of American *kolelim* may vary considerably, their students have a similar background. Virtually all are in their mid- to late twenties, graduates of postsecondary or *bet midrash* programs who, with few exceptions, have spent their academic careers within the confines of *yeshivot* in the United States or elsewhere, since the age of ten. By the time he enters the *kolel*, the student has mastered the methodology and the logic of Talmudic dialectics. Although the fellows arrive with similar training, their goals differ. Some intend to pursue careers as scholars and educators; others plan to enter the world of commerce or the professions. For these fellows, certain *kolelim* provide practical career options.

Most *kolel* fellows are married and have children. However, this is no longer the universal requirement it once was. Indeed, in some instances the married student is in the minority, and special accommodations are made for the single fellow, including informal matchmaking services. In many institutions, by contrast, only married applicants are considered for the programs.

The family context is an important aspect of *kolel* study. In many cases the student is the son or brother of a *kolel* alumnus and has made his academic choice on the basis of such influence. Parents and in-laws will frequently subsidize the fellow's income for the duration of his *kolel* study. Indeed, in many such cases a period of subsidized *kolel* study may have been part of a prenuptial agreement insisted upon by both bride and groom.

Wives of *kolel* families generally work outside the home, even though they may also be responsible for families of up to five children. Most attest to the importance of *kolel* study in cementing their family relations and lending them structure and stability. They take great pride in their husband's vocation and aspire to a similar goal for their children.

Career goals upon graduation are somewhat problematic. For most fellows, *kolel* study will last three to five years and by its very nature will not lead to a specific skill or profession. Nevertheless, a career in Jewish education, the rabbinate, or communal work is implicit in the course of study. Most students aspire to senior positions in secondary or postsecondary institutions. Such openings are quite limited, however, and competition is keen. Yet there does not appear to be much thought given to the matter of placement, and little is done to consider professional options. Both students and administration are content to "let the Lord provide."

Accountability

In many ways the description of how *kolel* fellows are evaluated and held accountable for their progress is one of the more troublesome aspects of the *kolel* as an educational institution. In most cases, accountability is extremely informal, as there are no written examinations, oral presentations, or dissertations to defend. Although absence and punctuality are recorded, there is generally no penalty for poor attendance beyond counseling and peer pressure. Records are haphazardly kept and, with notable exception, standards are not clearly articulated nor objectives defined.

In most cases, evaluation and accountability are left to the devices of the *rosh hakolel,* the *mashgi' ah,* or both, and they are expected to know each fellow personally, meet with him regularly, and discuss any difficulties or shortcomings he may experience. In addition, the influence of study partners and *haburah* colleagues is also expected to serve as a motivating force in encouraging the weaker fellows to maintain minimum standards of attendance and study.

Certain *kolelim* have more systematically confronted the issue. Some have devised nontraditional, highly material incentives to increase motivation and penalize inadequate performance. Regular written examinations have been introduced as well as supplements to monthly stipends linked to the students' scores. Additional grants are made available for extra-credit work, and students can add handily to their income by displaying their competence in this formal manner. By the same token, those who do poorly receive no such supplements, and continued poor performance will result in suspension from the *kolel*.

The foregoing has been but a brief introduction to the American *kolel*, its structure, academic programs, students, and faculty. The chapters that follow detail the variations suggested above and offer a much fuller picture of the continuity and change that the *kolel* represents in higher Jewish education. It is appropriate that we undertake this study within the context of the following remarks made by the *rosh yeshivah* of Yeshiva Ner Israel of Baltimore:

> Present the case for the *kolel* as strongly as you can for two important reasons. Firstly, the *kolel* program has already proven itself and has produced extraordinary Torah scholars. They are taking their rightful place as *Roshei Yeshivah*, rabbis of communities, principals of day schools and pioneers of new communities.
>
> Secondly, the *kolel* needs to be projected to the generous supporters of Torah in America and elsewhere. We can and do raise tremendous sums of money for the support of *yeshivos ketanos* [elementary level *yeshivot*]. But it is very difficult to raise funds for a *kolel*. The *ba'alei battim* [laymen] have not yet accepted the *kolel* as an absolute necessity for the future growth of Torah.[12]

PART TWO
The Kolelim

1. THE RABBI AARON KOTLER INSTITUTE
FOR ADVANCED LEARNING
OF BETH MEDRASH GOVOHA

Beth Medrash Govoha of Lakewood, New Jersey, houses the largest *kolel* in the United States.* It enrolls 474 fellows from ten states and from fourteen foreign countries. In addition, there are 470 students registered in various other divisions of the institution. Having begun with a student body of only twelve at the time of its inception, the growth of Beth Medrash Govoha and its impact upon postwar Jewish life are most impressive.[1]

Its development is largely a tribute to the work of its founder, R. Aaron Kotler (1891–1962). R. Kotler arrived in the United States in 1941 as a result of special visa and asylum privileges granted by President Roosevelt to a select group of scholars in various fields of intellectual endeavor. He had previously served as the assistant and later as director of the Yeshiva Ez Hayyim of Kletsk, a position that he held for twenty years prior to his arrival in America.

As such, he was recognized throughout the Jewish world for his scholarship, teaching methods, and forceful leadership. Of particular note was his interest in and concern for Jewish education. Indeed, prior to his emi-

---

*Information regarding the number of students, faculty, stipends and salaries at the Beth Medrash Govoha is based on interviews conducted in 1982.

gration, he helped establish a *kolel* in Monsey, New York, during a visit on behalf of his *yeshivah*.[2]

In April 1943, R. Kotler established the Beth Medrash Govoha in Lakewood, New Jersey, after an earlier attempt in New Rochelle, New York, did not succeed. The student body consisted of twelve promising graduates of American rabbinical schools who were attracted by the reputation of R. Kotler and sought his tutelage. In 1945, R. Kotler was joined by fifteen young men who had been his students in Europe. These war refugees had crossed the Soviet Union eastward and remained in Japan and Shanghai for the war's duration.[3]

The institution they formed was named Beth Medrash Govoha (Advanced Study Hall). Its title reflected R. Kotler's intention to create a school whose alumni would ultimately establish a network of *yeshivot* in America and help raise the standards of existing institutions of higher Torah study. To this day, the institution remains true to those goals.

During his tenure as director of the Beth Medrash Govoha, R. Kotler served as President of the Council of Torah Sages, the supreme religious body of Agudath Israel (Union of Israel), a world orthodox movement and political party. As such, he was broadly recognized as the leader of the militantly traditional "right wing" of American Judaism. He was also instrumental in forming the Va'ad ha-Hatzalah, a commission whose avowed purpose was to rescue and aid refugees from the European Holocaust of World War II, and Hinukh Azma'i, Israel's independent religious educational system.

Kolel Structure

The *kolel*, named after its founder, is officially called the Rabbi Aaron Kotler Institute for Advanced Learning. It is located on a large campus in suburban Lakewood, New Jersey, about 65 miles southeast of New York City. Covering some nine acres, the campus provides a large study hall, conference and seminar rooms, classrooms, lecture halls, and dining facilities. Three separate libraries house a collection of some 10,000 volumes of Talmudic, rabbinic, and classical Jewish studies available for student use. In addition, a microfilm and audiotape collection has recently been added to supplement these holdings.[4]

Admission to the *kolel* is based upon letters of reference, an oral examination (usually with a younger member of the faculty), and an interview with the dean of admissions. The oral examination generally revolves around the applicant's recent Talmudic studies, although proficiency in the Bible, philosophy, and classical Hebrew is officially required. Letters from the applicant's most recent instructors and the evaluation of the dean of admission are also part of the final decision.[5]

Observation suggests, however, that if the applicant is an alumnus of the lower division of Beth Medrash Govoha, then the application procedure is largely a formality. Entry into the *kolel* is virtually assured. An undergraduate of inferior ability would normally be discouraged from applying, but the superior student is usually invited to join the *kolel* upon graduation.

Kolel students may be married or single and may remain at the *kolel* for two to ten years, though there is no formal residency requirement. Generally, those who stay longest intend to pursue careers in the rabbinate or Jewish education, whereas those who remain only a few years will enter business or the professions. Their years at the *kolel* are generally intended for personal growth and satisfaction and, at times, for enhancing their status.

Kolel fellows receive a weekly stipend of $40. This may be supplemented by a work-study program and a special scholarship fund for particularly needy students. Students may also apply for a variety of financial-assistance, grant, and loan programs operated by the federal government. Wives generally work outside the home as teachers in local Hebrew schools or elementary *yeshivot*, as computer programmers, or as clerical workers. Parents and in-laws often subsidize the student's income, and the *kolel* administration will frequently serve as the intermediary to facilitate or augment these arrangements. The *kolel* does not encourage students to seek part-time or freelance employment outside the institution.[6]

Beth Medrash Govoha provides subsidized living accommodations for its married *kolel* fellows. The *yeshivah* owns 80 two- and three-bedroom garden apartments in close proximity to its campus. These are apportioned on a first-come, first-served basis and cost the student between $200 and $350 per month, with the balance subsidized by the *yeshivah*. Some married students prefer to live off campus, and several own homes in the area.

The presence of the Beth Medrash Govoha has had a profound impact upon the local Jewish community, despite the fact that the *yeshivah* constitutes its own insular community and students do not participate in local activities to any appreciable degree. The demand for kosher products and religious services has increased because of the greater availability. There has been a conspicuous rise in religious observances, encouraging many peripheral Jews to become more committed.

Kolel wives serve on the faculty of local day schools or synagogue Hebrew schools and instill their religious perspectives and values in the children of the community. Most important, the *yeshivah* has founded a *heder* (elementary Jewish parochial school) which now enrolls some 800 children. In 1971 The Talmudic High School of Central New Jersey was established in nearby Adelphia. The curriculum, faculty, and standards of these two schools operate in close relation with the parent institution.

In describing the influence of Beth Medrash Govoha upon the Jewish community of Lakewood, R. Pesach Levovitz, spiritual leader of a local congregation, noted:

> Until fifteen years ago, Lakewood was a town known for its resort hotels and as an egg-producing center. Now it is a world-famous Torah center and the community has a Sabbath-observant bakery for the first time. . . . It is a very interesting phenomenon to see hundreds of men wearing *talesim* [prayer shawls], walking to and from the synagogues on the Sabbath.[7]

Program of Study

Students at the R. Aaron Kotler Institute attend sessions six days a week. On Fridays, sessions are abbreviated to allow the students time for Sabbath preparations. The academic year begins on the first of Elul (August) and ends before Tisha B'Av (mid-July). The academic calendar provides for vacations during the entire month of Nisan (March–April) in which Passover falls, and from Yom Kippur until the week following the Sukkot Festival (mid-October).

A typical day of studies at the *kolel* reflects a rigorous schedule as well as the considerable independence fellows are permitted. Morning prayers begin at 7:40 and are followed by a *seder* from 9:30 A.M. to 1:45 P.M. A second *seder* follows lunch, from 3:45 to 7:30, with a break for dinner at 6:30 P.M. From 7:30 to 8:00, students typically take off time from Talmudic analysis and devote it to *musar*. This is followed by a night *seder* until 9:15 taken either at the study hall or in the students' homes. Students make time for afternoon and evening prayers.[8]

Like most other subjects of this study, the fellows of the Rabbi Aaron Kotler Institute study in pairs. In addition, each belongs to a *haburah*, an intellectually and socially compatible group of eight to ten students that operates with considerable independence. These groups are formed voluntarily and are free to choose their own texts, study topics, schedule, and depth of analysis, in coordination with a faculty member.

Within the *haburot*, a rotation is maintained so that each student has the opportunity and obligation to direct the sessions periodically. The particular student is responsible for preparing the relevant texts and commentaries for presentation to his colleagues. It is their task to analyze and challenge his presentation, forcing him to document, support, and possibly modify his position. A student who is unable to prepare adequately or who is frequently found to be wanting may be asked to seek another *haburah* closer to his intellectual level. It is not uncommon for students to change *haburot* during the course of stay at the *kolel*.[9]

In addition, the entire *yeshivah* attends lectures presented by the *rosh yeshivah* twice each week. Until his death in 1983, R. Shneur Kotler, R. Aaron's son, served in that capacity. These sessions deal with the particular Talmudic text studied by the *yeshivah* generally, which is typically one tractate of an eight-year annual cycle. Regardless of the particular topics covered by a *haburah*, members attend these lectures for the insights to be gleaned as well as the intellectual enjoyment.

Faculty and senior fellows are also assigned to assist the younger and less erudite of the *haburot* and frequently lead their study sessions. At times, a *rosh haburah* may be appointed to offer a series of lectures revolving about the particular topics discussed by the *rosh yeshivah* or other visiting scholars. His is a position of particular status defined as

> a scholar-in-residence, one of a group of senior fellows who are completely "on their own" in their individual and academic pursuits. They are part of the Beth Medrash Govoha community and study and work regularly in the same study halls and libraries. The *Rosh Haburah* supplements the lectures of the professorate and visiting scholars through regular lectures and seminars and colloquia.[10]

The Rabbi Aaron Kotler Institute confers rabbinic ordination upon *kolel* students who pursue a specified course of study. Ordination is not required of fellows, and application is made by the entire *haburah* rather than by the individual. Following six years of study, the *haburah* may elect to study those relevant sections of the Talmud and the classical codes leading to the rabbinic degree. Upon completion, the student is examined by one of several rabbinic authorities, often from outside the faculty. If found qualified, he will receive his diploma from the institution.[11]

Faculty

The faculty of the *yeshivah* consists of its director, 16 professors and associate professors, a *mashgi'ah*, and 3 assistants. It appears that of the 16 faculty members, 5 devote their work specifically to *kolel* programs. The counseling staff is available for consultation on an individual and informal basis. In addition, they deliver regular lectures on topics in Jewish philosophy and ethics. The institution also lists 12 administrative and 6 academic officers.

Beyond its formal staff, the *kolel* also supports 37 scholars-in-residence, senior fellows whose responsibilities have been outlined above. More recently, a "buddy system" has been introduced. Older students are asked to work with younger *kolel* fellows or students in other divisions of the *yeshivah* in need of remedial aid or personal support. Undertaken on a voluntary basis, this program occasionally supplants the fellow's own studies.

Students

The typical fellow of the Beth Medrash Govoha *kolel* is between the ages of 21 to 40, is married, and has two or three children. As noted, there are 474 such fellows, making this the largest program of its kind in the United States. Indeed, even this number is deceptive, for there are few clear differentiations between *kolel* students and those in the undergraduate divisions, particularly in terms of curriculum and methods of study.

> In actuality there are no clear lines of division between the yeshivah students and the kolel fellows in the grouping arrangements. The kolel fellows are identified by the fact that they receive a stipend.[12]

As might be expected, because of the size of the institution, there is considerable diversity among the students, both in backgrounds and levels of preparation. The *haburah* system described above tends to reinforce these variations, though not to the point of exclusivity. As a result, certain symbolically important concessions have had to be made.

For example, in the Beth Medrash Govoha, which is a direct descendant of the Lithuanian *yeshivah* tradition, and whose founder was the *rosh yeshivah* of Kletsk, one might hardly expect a substantially *hasidic* presence.* Nevertheless, it is estimated that almost 30 percent of the student body is of *hasidic* background, upbringing, and demeanor. *Hasidic* thought is studied on a voluntary basis each day, and there appears to be no conflict or tension between these students and their colleagues.

These variations notwithstanding, a common thread does emerge among students in regard to their aspirations and intentions. For the most part, study in the *kolel* is not undertaken as professional preparation leading to a specific career. Rather, it is felt that one who leaves his religious studies after secondary or even undergraduate preparation is somehow "unfinished," and that this inadequacy will be reflected both in his personal life and in his contribution to the Jewish community.

---

*Originally, the emergence of the *hasidic* movement in Eastern Europe was not warmly received by learned Lithuanian rabbis, who were known as *misnagdim* (opponents). This tension has diminished considerably.

Kolel students seem to uphold the view that the Jewish community requires laymen who are genuine scholars to assure its well-being; indeed, this view is part of the general mission of the institution. Those who know but a "smattering" are dilettantes whose contribution will be of little value. The following observation was made by a student:

> *Klal Yisrael* needs people who know all of the Torah, its philosophy, and particularly its laws. In order to maintain and safeguard the Jewish people in the future, we need to fulfill Rav Aaron Kotler's prophecy, that America can produce a Torah community to replace the destroyed generation of Europe. It is necessary to learn and, in Lakewood, it is felt that even the student who does not achieve the ultimate goal of becoming a Torah giant will be a prominent *baal habaws* [layman].[13]

The point is confirmed in discussions with *kolel* wives and their children. There appears to be a general consensus among the wives that joining the *kolel* has strengthened their marriages and created special bonds that reinforce the relationship. The *kolel* fellow is held in great esteem by his wife, since in most cases she sought such a spouse and, at times, even made such a stipulation prior to the marriage. Children are said to respect their fathers for the sacrifice and commitment they have made and for the importance of their contribution to Jewish life. A son is raised to follow in his father's path and become a *kolel* student himself, and a daughter is encouraged to marry one. Interestingly, most students of the *kolel* have close relatives who have studied at Beth Medrash Govoha or in similar institutions elsewhere.[14]

For its part, the *yeshivah* does encourage its students to consider careers in communal service, the rabbinate, and particularly in Jewish education. Joint seminars are conducted with Torah Umesorah, the National Association of Jewish Day Schools. An internship program has been developed that allows *kolel* fellows to teach at elementary *yeshivot* in and around Lakewood, and a variety of practica have been established to provide the student with "hands-on" experience.[15]

Such programs include apprenticeship courses at local slaughterhouses for those interested in becoming *shohetim* (ritual slaughterers). Students may also train under the direction of a certified *mohel* (circumciser) if they aspire to such certification. Such programs also exist for those interested in ritual calligraphy, in preparation for practice as *soferim*, scribes of *tephillin*, *mezuzot*, and religious documents that must be written by hand.

The institution has also embarked on a vigorous outreach program, motivated in large measure by the desire to expand the opportunities available to its graduates. As early as 1952, R. Aaron Kotler established the Pioneer

Scholarship Program to prepare fellows for careers on the faculty of high schools and programs of higher learning. Branch schools have been founded by graduates of the Beth Medrash Govoha in such diverse locations as Philadelphia, St. Louis, Denver, and Stamford.

In addition, an innovative Community Kolel Program has been undertaken in which young alumni have founded postgraduate programs in various cities, aimed at full participation in and development of adult education, communal service, and outreach within the locality. The first such *kolel* was created in Toronto in 1970, and was followed by similar institutions in Detroit, Los Angeles, Pittsburgh, Chicago, and Melbourne, Australia. Each is largely staffed by graduates of the Beth Medrash Govoha and sees itself as a shadow of the original institution. The Los Angeles *kolel* is discussed in detail elsewhere in this study, as a model of this phenomenon.

Aside from reaching out to those areas where higher Jewish education is inaccessible, Beth Medrash Govoha has also offered an opportunity for alumni and others to enter its world for a brief venture into pure Torah study. An annual summer retreat has been established at its campus, utilizing faculty, students, and other available resources. Known as the *Yarhei Kallah* Retreat and modeled after a similar practice developed in Talmudic times, this is an intensive, two-week program of lectures, independent research, and study intended to parallel the regular program of study in a condensed format.[16]

Kolel fellows participate as faculty and aides, attending to administrative matters, providing programmatic assistance, and helping to develop the curriculum. Child care is available, as are voluntary sessions for the wives of these visitors. This offers the fellow a further opportunity to develop his educational and administrative skills, while helping to reinforce the commitments of others to advanced Jewish learning.

Finally, Beth Medrash Govoha has created the SEED (Summer Education Environmental Development) Program in coordination with Torah Umesorah. Here, *kolel* fellows are sponsored by a Jewish community in some area inaccessible to traditional Jewish education. It is their responsibility

> to pursue a special study course for several weeks in the summer, providing the host community the inspiring opportunity of participation in lectures, seminars and prayer sessions within the framework of a microcosmic *yeshivah*.[17]

The program was founded in 1974 and has sent groups of students to far-flung communities throughout North and Central America. More recently, students from other *yeshivot* have been invited to participate in collaboration with their own educational programs.

Aside from the structural and programmatic aspects of student life at Beth Medrash Govoha, most notable is the spiritual environment that has been created there. Students are encouraged to bring their study into practice through ritual and prayer, which they do with intense feeling and tangible commitment. Religious services and holiday rites are conducted by students, and their close relationships are apparent in this phase of daily activity.

In addition, the relationship between the student, *rosh yeshivah*, and *mashgi'ah* is very close, and a student can seek personal spiritual guidance from any faculty member. Faculty members are far more than lecturers who deliver a discourse and leave. They are, rather, spiritual mentors and role models who take their responsibility very seriously. The nature of the school and the personality of the faculty members are responsible for this.[18]

Moreover, the personality of R. Shneur Kotler, son and successor of the institution's founder, contributed immensely to the warmth and intimacy of the *yeshivah*, despite its size. His personal sincerity and friendliness made him a beloved figure. (R. Shneur died as this book was being researched, and a successor has not yet emerged (1985) from among four leading candidates. The impact of his loss upon the institution is yet to be assessed.)

Ironically, despite the intensity of their feelings for the institution during their stay there, the fellows upon becoming alumni have not been active in support of the school until very recently. It is worth noting that most of those who have entered commercial or professional careers dedicate as much as ten to fifteen hours per week to the pursuit of Jewish studies on their own. Those who reside in proximity to others of like mind have occasionally joined to conduct their own religious services or hold study sessions.

Recently there has been a campaign to organize the alumni and keep them involved. An alumni newsletter appeared in 1977 but was interrupted and then revived in 1981. A center of alumni activity was established in New York, the Alumni Beth Medrash Govoha Study Hall at 5109 16th Avenue, Brooklyn, New York. Regular classes are held there, as well as guest lectures. A smaller facility was created in Monsey, New York, where a retreat is organized for alumni and faculty each year. The program includes lectures, study sessions, and the opportunity for fellowship on a basis similar to the *Yarhei Kallah* retreats described above.[19]

Two areas of concern, curriculum and accountability, have been the object of minor controversies in previous analyses of the Beth Medrash Govoha. With regard to curriculum, one study concludes that a key to the school's success is the study of *musar:*

> *Musar* is studied by the faculty and students of Beth Medrash Govoha. . . .
> The success of Rabbi Aaron Kotler in training American youths to Torah
> should not be ignored. The *Musar* process is successful on the level of higher
> Jewish education, to gain Torah commitment.[20]

Yet no such emphasis emerged from the present investigation. *Musar* is
given but fleeting recognition in the studies of *kolel* students and by no
means occupies an important part of their schedules. Only about thirty
minutes each day are devoted to the study of *musar*, and lectures on the
topic are not fully attended. R. Kotler and his successors have certainly
had great success. However, it is difficult to attribute this success to the
place of *musar* in the school's curriculum or objectives.

Accountability

As with other subjects of this study, there are few formal means by
which to evaluate the progress and success of given students at the *kolel* of
Beth Medrash Govoha. As noted before, there are no formal examinations, no residency requirements, no theses or dissertations to research,
and no oral defense of independent or group studies before a faculty committee.

The matter has led one writer to criticize the *yeshivah* and its program
for certain flaws that can be easily found in similar institutions elsewhere.
He contends that students at the Beth Medrash Govoha are left

> for the most part to fend for themselves, poring over their books for hours on
> end in one of the several crowded, noisy study halls. Since there are no formal
> classes at Lakewood, any two students who get along well together and who are
> able to study together in a compatible fashion are free to form a *hevrutah*. Stu-
> dents are also free to request permission to substitute alternative tractates for
> the ones that have been assigned for study each semester. To cap things off,
> there are no examinations at Lakewood and no such thing as graduation.[21]

While many of the objective conditions he describes are accurate, the
criticism may be too pointed. Indeed, there are no formal examinations,
but the *haburah* system assures that students will be required to lead group
sessions periodically. Such a responsibility forces the student to research
and organize intelligent presentations, defending them from the attacks of
his colleagues and anticipating their criticism. Peer pressure can be a far
more important motivation for success than regular examinations or close
faculty supervision.

Moreover, the very freedom and flexibility of the *kolel* have been considered part of the great strengths and attractions of the institution. A student need not compete for grades, honors, or awards, but may seek his own intellectual and social level in the pursuit of *Torah lishmah*, Torah study for its own sake. The avowed aim of the institution is life-long study. Thus, the implicit "completion" of one's studies through examinations and graduation is naturally absent in a school of this kind. Finally, one cannot overestimate the power of the close and warm relationship that exists between students, faculty, counselors, and scholars-in-residence, which ensures that the typical fellow of the *kolel* at Beth Medrash Govoha is not left "to fend for himself" at all.

Having said this, it is equally clear that no objective means of student evaluation exists there, nor is there likely to be such a development. Motivation is expected from within, and there is no penalty for poor performance beyond that of social pressure. In the words of one administrator, "the failure in Lakewood becomes the pious, learned layman in his community."[22]

2. MIRRER YESHIVA CENTRAL INSTITUTE

Though it is difficult to set a precise date for the founding of the Yeshiva of Mir, it is likely that the institution opened its doors during the second decade of the nineteenth century in the town of Grodno Oblast, in what is now the Belorussian S.S.R. The *yeshivah* was founded by R. Samuel Tiktinski, who maintained it at his own expense, delivering *shi'urim* there for eight years. He was succeeded by his son R. Abraham, who died childless soon after. A period of conflict ensued, involving the rabbi of the town, R. Joseph David Eisenstadt, his own son R. Moses Abraham, and R. Hayyim Leib Tiktinski, another son of the founder. Through the intervention of R. Isaac Elhonen Spector, R. Hayyim Tiktinski was appointed director of the *yeshivah* in 1856.[23]

For the first century of its existence, the *yeshivah* was largely supported by local laymen who exercised considerable authority over internal matters, save for the method and content of learning. With the death of R. Hayyim Leib Tiktinski in 1899, a period of transition ensued. Under the direction of R. Eli Barukh Kamai, appointed R. Tiktinski's successor in 1901, the *yeshivah* attained its independence from local leaders and moved away from the tradition of *musar*. The institution flourished until World War II. On its staff served such well-known luminaries as R. Shimon Skop, R. Eliezer

Yehuda Finkel, son-in-law and successor to R. Kamai, and R. Yeruham Levovitz.

The nature and method of study at the *yeshivah* underwent several changes as a result of both internal and external influences. During its early period, students would study in groups round the clock and lectures were delivered by the *rosh yeshivah* four times a week. Emphasis was placed primarily upon textual analysis and the study of standard commentaries. An emphasis on *halakhah* (Jewish law) was introduced with the accession of R. Kamai in 1901. Though the study of *musar* was anathema during this period, it was introduced on a broad scale under the leadership of R. Finkel in 1909. Thus, the great Lithuanian tradition of intellectual scholarship merged with the emotional and pious strains of the *musar* movement that R. Finkel had imbibed during his years as a student at the *yeshivah* at Slobodka.

In the years following World War I and the Russian Revolution, R. Finkel, joined by R. Levovitz in 1924, shifted the direction of the institution from *harifut* to *beki' ut*. Prizes were awarded for mastering four major tractates in one year, and the shift was encouraged by groups of Mir students who took brief leave to study with R. Velvel of Brisk.

Indeed, it was through such exchanges that new intellectual influences were introduced to the *yeshivah*. Students were attracted to the *yeshivah* from Grodno, Radun, Kaminez, and Kletsk, and each brought with him the unique methods of such scholars as R. Shimon Skop, R. Barukh Ber Lebowitz, and R. Naftali of Radun. In addition, students from Poland, Western Europe, and the United States were attracted to this Torah center, making the Mirrer Yeshiva one of the most famous in Europe during the 1930s.

The leadership of the *yeshivah* was also charged with the full financial burden of maintaining the institution and supporting—in part or in full—many of its students. Fund-raising efforts were essential, and R. Finkel traveled to America in the mid-1920s, accompanied by R. Abraham Kalmanowitz, to seek support from the Jewish community there. The former returned to the *yeshivah* in 1936, while R. Kalmanowitz remained in America as president of the Mirrer Yeshiva until 1938.[24]

The advent of World War II signaled dark years for the Mirrer Yeshiva, as it did for Europe's entire Jewish community. R. Kalmanowitz returned to Europe to transfer the *yeshivah* to Vilna in 1939. He immigrated to America the following year and maneuvered the *yeshivah*'s move eastward first to Kobe, Japan, and later to Shanghai, China, where it remained in safety until 1945. The institution was then transferred in part to Jerusalem and in part to Brooklyn, where it was reopened in 1946 as the

Mirrer Yeshiva Central Institute. R. Abraham Kalmanowitz died in 1964 and was succeeded by his son, R. Shrage Moshe Kalmanowitz, and his son-in-law, R. Shmuel Berenbaum.

Kolel Structure

The Mirrer Yeshiva in America began in a small congregation in the Flatbush section of Brooklyn. By 1982 it comprised four buildings near the original site. The buildings currently house a high school, dormitory, rabbinical college, and administrative offices. The *kolel* began with 35 students and has now grown to 119, most of whom are graduates of the institution's lower division; about 20 percent of the students are from other institutions.

The typical Mir *kolel* fellow is in his late twenties, is married, and has three to five children. Though the majority are local students, the *kolel* has attracted fellows from five foreign countries and ten states, and claims to have graduated 1,000 students since 1947.[25]

The physical facilities of the *yeshivah* include a large *bet midrash*, which also serves as a synagogue; various classrooms; and a library housing some 10,000 volumes. In addition, there are two kitchens, a dining hall, and offices for the administration and faculty. The *yeshivah* also contains a gymnasium, though this is not regularly used by the *kolel* students.

Candidates for admission to the Mir Yeshiva *kolel* are evaluated by several standards. The principal criterion is academic suitability. Candidates are expected to have graduated from Talmudic high schools as well as a *bet midrash* program, and to have demonstrated distinction in their prior studies.

In addition, they must show evidence of personal commitment and motivation to pursue a rigorous program of Torah study. This often requires letters of recommendation from previous school authorities or from recognized members of the Orthodox rabbinate. In terms of achievement, candidates are officially expected to possess a thorough knowledge of the Bible and a mastery of a minimum of 150 folio pages of Talmud. Finally, they must display competence in the basic laws and customs of traditional Jewish life and a personal commitment to their observance.

Candidates apply in writing for admission and are expected to appear for personal interviews and an oral examination. Under certain circumstances, remedial work is indicated. Upon admission, students are eligible for monthly stipends of $160 to $400, depending upon ability and need. In addition, they may apply for several government aid programs to subsidize their income and housing. Each is free to make his own living arrangements.[26]

The presence of the Mirrer Yeshiva and its *kolel* has had a substantial impact upon the surrounding community. It is estimated that over 100 *kolel* families live in the immediate environs, which appears to have helped stabilize the ethnic and demographic composition of the area. In addition, the *yeshivah* takes pride in having been the first of its kind in Flatbush and in having "laid the foundation" for the provision of the supporting services considered essential for the development of a flourishing Orthodox Jewish community. It also points to its influence upon the large Sephardic Jewish community of Flatbush, many of whose leaders "have received their Torah guidance" from the Mirrer Yeshiva.[27]

In addition, the institution has joined regularly with other Orthodox community groups to foster and advance the place of Jewish values in the local community. An annual Sabbath-observance campaign has attracted both students and faculty of the *yeshivah*. Their students participated in a series of demonstrations aimed at closing a local pornographic establishment. The influence of the Mirrer Yeshiva upon Jewish life in Flatbush is confirmed by the fact that it maintains generally good relations with the local rabbinic leadership. The words of the president of the Rabbinic Board of Flatbush are instructive:

> The *Yeshivah* and *Kolel* have had a profound influence on the surrounding community. Mir was the first *yeshivah* of its kind in the neighborhood and the interaction between the *yeshivah* families and the local people has produced many positive Torah advances.[28]

Program of Study

Students of the Mir *kolel* attend sessions five days a week from 10:00 A.M. to 8:00 P.M. and on Fridays until early afternoon. The day is divided into three units. The morning *seder* extends from 10:00 A.M. until 2:00 P.M., followed by a break from 2:00 to 4:00 P.M. The afternoon *seder* follows from 4:00 to 8:00 P.M. The evening *seder* is generally conducted at home from 9:00 to 11:30 P.M. and includes study with a younger student of the *yeshivah* assigned for tutelage by the dean. The school year begins on the first of Elul (August or September) and ends on the first of Av (July or August); vacations are taken during holiday periods and the month of Av.

The primary course of study is directed toward the so-called "*yeshivah*" tractates in eight annual cycles: Bava Batra, Sanhedrin, Ketubot, Gittin, Pesahim, and Hullin. The curricular emphasis is clearly upon Talmud and its commentaries. However, some time is spent in regular courses dealing with weekly Torah readings, *musar*, and Jewish law.

Fellows spend time in study with a *hevrutah*. By far the most important influence in the content and structure of the student's work, however, is his membership in a *haburah*.[29] There are three such *haburot* at the Mir *kolel*. One *haburah* studies the same tractate as the *yeshivah* generally, according to its eight-year cycle. Members of the *haburah* study as a group and attend two lectures a week delivered on a rotating basis by R. Shmuel Berenbaum and by a member of the *haburah*.

The second group studies a tractate from the Talmudic section of Kodashim, which deals with ritual and service in the ancient Temple. Here the members elect a *rosh haburah* chosen for his scholastic ability, and it is his responsibility to lecture to the group on a periodic basis. In addition, other members of the *haburah* are invited to deliver such lectures, which may take place approximately once a week.

The third group studies a Talmudic tractate chosen from the Mo'ed section, which deals with the laws and customs of the Sabbath and Jewish holidays. Here too, a leader is elected, and lecture assignments are divided between him and other members of the group. It should be noted that such lecture sessions are not passive affairs. Students question and refute the presentation vigorously and take time to review each of its elements. Members of *haburot* may change from group to group, but only at the beginning of a new semester.

In addition to the *haburah*, fellows may join one of the *va'adim*, groups that meet regularly to study *musar* before afternoon and evening prayers. At this time the *mashgi'ah* or his designee will deliver a brief lecture based upon one of the classical *musar* texts, generally either *Hovot Halevavot* by Bahya ibn Pakudah or *Hokhmah U'musar* by Simcha Zisel Levovitz of Kelm. Attendance at such sessions is voluntary and quite low.

Indeed, despite the aforementioned importance of *musar* during the early period of the institution's development, it appears to play a minimal role today. This may be related to the absence of effective leadership capable of transmitting the inspirational message of *musar* to the present generation of students. In the words of one informant:

> Before R. Finkel or Reb Yehezkel gave a *musar shmu'es*, they prepared for 3 hours and then, they engaged their entire beings into the *shmu'es*. The venerated *mashgi'ah*, R. Tzvi Hirsch Feldman, put his entire heart into a *musar* discourse, and there has been no equal replacement since he died in 1976.[30]

Kolel students of advanced standing have the option of applying for rabbinic ordination. This requires a major examination of the candidate by a faculty board. Included on this panel are R. Berenbaum and R. Kalmanowitz, the *roshei yeshivah* who comprise the *kolel* faculty, as well as a *mashgi'ah* and a *rosh haburah*.

Faculty

The faculty of the Mirrer Yeshiva are all recognized scholars. In addition, many trace their lineage to the founders of the institution in America. They spend most of their time delivering lectures and supervising students on an individual basis. Raising funds for the *yeshivah* is a small but important part of their responsibilities.

The average faculty salary is ca. $18,500 per year plus health benefits. At present, there is no retirement or disability plan. However, owing to the passing of two faculty members whose widows receive their full salaries, such a plan is presently under consideration.[31]

Students

As indicated, the majority of the students are graduates of the Mirrer High School and Bet Midrash. They come from families of either Lithuanian, *hasidic*, or Sephardic background and in some instances of mixed background. Ninety-five percent are American-born, and sixty-five percent have relatives who have studied in a *kolel* in either the United States or Israel. The vast majority wear beards, expose their *tzizit* (fringes), and do not pursue university education.

A central motivation is the desire to devote full time to one's studies even after marriage, a proposition that is financially feasible only within the *kolel* program. The aspiration of such students is allegedly the attainment of the informal title "*lamdan*," loosely translated as scholar of broad erudition. In the words of one student of the Mirrer *kolel*:

> It requires full-time participation to achieve this goal. The *kolel* also gives a new *derekh* [way or system] in learning because it provides an opportunity to offer a presentation to *haburot* and thus gain practical experience in teaching others.[32]

As noted, the typical *kolel* family has three to five children. Family relations are apparently influenced by the fact that a *kolel* student is perceived to have reached a measure of status and esteem in the community as a scholar and as an individual of high ethical standards. This, it is claimed, influences both husband and wife to maintain a peaceful home that reflects Torah values.[33] The children are brought up in homes without television and comic books and, therefore, are not exposed to the general culture, which is considered anathema. Mir *kolel* fathers unanimously state that they look forward to the time when their sons will join a *kolel*, preferably their alma mater.

With regard to career aspirations, Mir *kolel* fellows interviewed uniformly noted the desire to serve on the faculty of upper-level *yeshivot*. They seem confident that a substantial number of such positions will be available to them and that the field is an expanding one. A typical response is most revealing:

> The birth rate among *yeshivah* families is much higher than the average in the United States. We expect that the population will cause increases in the number of *yeshivos* and classes, necessitating more teachers and *rebbeim*. Furthermore, there will be a need for more specialization in the future. Parents will demand smaller classes so that children can receive a maximum Torah education. Those who are *re'uyim*, fit, will become the *roshei yeshivah* throughout the world.[34]

In addition, some opportunities have become available to Mir *kolel* graduates as a result of a recent outreach program undertaken by the institution. Mir has not been in the forefront of these programs, in comparison with the Beth Medrash Govoha of Lakewood, Ner Israel of Baltimore, and Hafez Hayyim of Queens. Nevertheless, since 1979, a concerted effort has been made to develop contacts with distant Jewish communities and place *kolel* graduates in educational positions therein. Most notable is a program in which ten *kolel* graduates were sent to Mexico City at the request of the Mexican Jewish community. A similar group is presently being prepared for a trip to Panama. Nevertheless, when pressed about their plans for the future, most *kolel* students simply express their faith that the Lord will provide.

Within the *yeshivah* itself, one is impressed by its relaxed and noncompetitive spirit. Many of the *kolel* students return to the *bet midrash* after hours and study well past midnight. Those who live within walking distance also attend services at the *yeshivah* on the Sabbath and holidays. Indeed, increasing numbers of *kolel* students elect to live near the *yeshivah* and to remain there even after they conclude their studies at Mir.

Thus far, the Mir *kolel* has not established an official alumni organization and has depended upon informal peer networks and the strong loyalty of its graduates to maintain the relationship among alumni. Many have remained in the general area, where they continue to attend services and lectures at the *yeshivah* and visit with its faculty.

In addition, graduates participate in special fund-raising programs and generally support the activities of their alma mater. In 1978, alumni published the history of their institution to mark its thirtieth anniversary in America.[35] As evidence of their loyalty, many alumni send their own children to the elementary and high school programs at Mir.

Accountability

Assessing the level and effectiveness of study among the students of the Mirrer Kolel is not an easy task. On the one hand, there are no formal examinations or records save for absence and punctuality. No incentives have been instituted to motivate the student or penalize him for poor performance.

However, informal influences do exist to provide the necessary motivation, and the Mirrer Kolel relies heavily upon such factors. Thus, the faculty is always available to work with fellows, supervise their study, and serve as role models for their behavior. There is also notable peer pressure which, while not overbearing, tends to prevent sloth and idleness. A student's progress is also motivated by wives and family, who often suffer economic hardship to support the fellow's vocation and would be most distraught were his progress to falter. Therefore, the husband's moral responsibility is considerable. The Mirrer Kolel offers less financial support to its students than do other such institutions. The men who choose to study there must, therefore, be well motivated.

One is still left, however, with a system of loose accountability at best and very little precision in the assessment of a fellow's progress. While peer or family pressure may prevent gross lapses in scholarly activity—as do the requirements that the fellows prepare lectures and tutor younger students—the absence of a formal system of examination and evaluation must be considered a weakness.

In sum, the Mirrer Kolel is a typical example of such institutions in the United States. It is a unit of a major *yeshivah*, which traces its heritage back over 170 years to the great Torah centers of Lithuanian scholarship. It has graduated a substantial number of students, maintains a good relationship with its surrounding community, and has haltingly undertaken an outreach program both to promote Jewish values and help provide a vocational outlet for its graduates.

It is curious that almost no literature exists that describes the development of this institution or examines its impact upon American Jewish life. Joseph Epstein's lengthy article[36] is primarily historical and discusses the chronology of the institution from its founding in the 1800s through its transfer to the United States and Israel in 1945. Though valuable, it says little about the growth, structure, and development of the Mirrer Kolel since World War II.

Finally, Alvin Schiff, in his study of day school education in the United States, makes no mention of Mir as an institution of Jewish learning except to note the size of its graduating class and the number of Mir students who were New York State Regents Scholarship winners in 1963 and 1964.[37]

3. NER ISRAEL RABBINICAL COLLEGE

Ner Israel Rabbinical College was established in Baltimore, Maryland, in 1933 by R. Jacob I. Ruderman (1901-   ). R. Ruderman was trained at the *yeshivah* of Slabodka and in the *kolel* of Kovno. He arrived in the United States in 1930 and initially joined with R. Yehuda Levenberg on the faculty of the Bet Medrash LeRabbanim, then in Cleveland, a *yeshivah* that had been earlier established by his father-in-law, R. Sheftal Kramer.[38]

In 1933, R. Ruderman left Cleveland to found his own *yeshivah* in Baltimore. The institution received its charter from the State of Maryland in 1934 and opened its doors with fifteen students in their late teens. In 1944, R. Ruderman later helped create Torah Umesorah, the National Association of Jewish Day Schools, and served as chairman of its rabbinical advisory board. In 1961 he established a branch of Yeshiva Ner Israel in Toronto, which was directed by his son-in-law, R. Jacob Weinberg. Since 1963 the central institution has been authorized to confer rabbinic ordination as well as the degrees of Bachelor, Master, and Doctor of Talmudic Law.[39]

The *kolel* was also established in 1961 for the purpose of providing academic and moral training for young men who would later serve as rabbis and educators in the American Jewish community. At the time, there were ten students admitted to its program; that number had grown to fifty by 1982, and thirty fellows were subsidized by the institution in that year. The *kolel* is seen as an extension of the undergraduate institution and enables the fellow to pursue his studies independently, under the supervision of a faculty member.[40]

The *kolel* leaders perceive their function to be that of producing three types of graduates, according to their abilities and needs: (a) leading scholars who will serve as teachers and interpreters of Jewish law; (b) community leaders and pulpit rabbis who will "devote their lives to communal involvement although they are not of *rosh yeshivah* caliber";[41] and (c) those who plan to enter the professions and whose desire to study at the *kolel* is largely avocational. Nevertheless, their importance as future lay leaders makes their inclusion within the *kolel* important.

Kolel Structure

The entire *yeshivah* is housed in a complex of seven buildings in sub-urban Baltimore. These provide classrooms, dormitories, garden apartments for some married students and staff, kitchen and dining facilities, and various administrative offices. The *kolel* has its own *bet midrash* with smaller study rooms available as well. The library, which serves the entire *yeshivah*, is divided into three major collections.

The college library houses a broad collection of traditional Talmudic and Judaic works common to most large *yeshivot*. The *rosh yeshivah's* collection is heavily oriented toward periodicals and current responsa, with many volumes of Biblical commentaries and homiletic works. The collection attached to the graduate school includes works in Jewish history and philosophy as well as critical editions of many classical texts. The library presently contains over 16,000 volumes.

Applicants for admission to the Ner Israel Kolel must be graduates of recognized undergraduate *yeshivah* programs. They take an oral examination administered by the faculty and must show proficiency in Hebrew and Aramaic. In fact, most of the applicants are graduates of the Ner Israel high school or *bet midrash*. Students from other institutions generally bring references and endorsements from their faculty. All applicants must be married.[42]

Upon admission, students receive (1982) stipends of $50 per week plus an annual bonus of $1,000 for those with three or more children. In addition, work-study assignments are available, and students can supplement their income by $300 to $500 per year in this manner. Campus housing is subsidized, but there are far too few units available, and consequently about half the *kolel* families rent apartments elsewhere at monthly rates of about $400. Finally, students may apply for a variety of federal and state grants as well as loans and loan guarantee programs.

The presence of an institution such as the Ner Israel Yeshiva has had a marked impact upon the quality of Jewish life in Baltimore and its environs. Unlike similar institutions located within highly concentrated Jewish communities, Ner Israel is quite unusual in Baltimore. It can justifiably claim a primary role in attracting kosher establishments and institutions that provide particular services for Orthodox Jewish clientele. Its students and alumni have had a profound effect on the nature of primary and secondary Jewish education in the area, and both the integrity and stability of the local Jewish community have thus been enhanced.

In addition, the presence of the *yeshivah* has attracted many Jewish families, notably alumni and their relatives, to the community. Ner Israel attempts to cooperate with local rabbinical leaders in matters of mutual concern. A comprehensive outreach program intended to service local needs in the areas of education and youth work is described in detail below.

Program of Study

The students of the Ner Israel Kolel attend sessions for five-and-a-half days each week, although those who live on campus will frequently spend their free time in study as well. The day is divided into three sessions of unequal proportions. The morning unit follows prayers and generally extends from 9:30 A.M. to 1:00 P.M. The second session begins with afternoon prayers at 2:15 P.M., includes a *musar* lecture, and lasts until 3:00 P.M. Many of the *kolel* fellows use this time to study with younger students. The last session begins at 4:00 P.M. and continues until 6:30 P.M.; hence, the formal schedule ends somewhat earlier than in many other institutions.

There is no formal residency requirement, and tenure for a student at the *kolel* may be as little as three years or as many as ten, depending upon aspirations and ability. Those who plan to enter Jewish education, however, generally do not remain beyond five years.[43]

There are three *haburot* at Ner Israel. As of 1982, one group has been studying the Talmudic tractate Shabbat, while a second is linked to the text chosen for study by the entire *yeshivah* (Bava Kamma in 1983–84). The third *haburah*, however, is unique and deserves some explanation.

As noted, the *kolel* sees itself as an institution that must produce a variety of graduates, from learned laymen to great scholars. Those students who show promise of entering the latter ranks, i.e., of becoming great scholarly leaders and interpreters of the law, are placed in this third *haburah*. The curriculum for this group is exclusively limited to those Talmudic texts that are considered most relevant to the needs of one who will be called upon to render decisions in Jewish law. These generally include Eruvin, Hullin, Niddah, and Mikva'ot, among others.

In addition, this group of exceptional students, about twenty within the *kolel* (1982), is encouraged to follow in the footsteps of the *rosh yeshivah*, whose emphasis is on *beki'ut* rather than on the minutiae of a given page or section of the tractate.

The point is clearly articulated by the *rosh yeshivah* in his view of the training required to produce a competent *yeshivah* teacher:

> If someone is going to be a *rebbe* in a *yeshivah* and he will say a *shiur*, he should be prepared to answer questions to the students from the entire tractate and not only from the page being studied. A broad knowledge of Talmud is imperative to be a good Talmud teacher.[44]

In general, these *haburot* operate independently and at their own pace. By design, the students are allowed to advance in tune with their needs and to meet with R. Weinberg, the second major faculty member after R. Ruderman, or with R. Eisseman, the *mashgi'ah*. The former delivers a lecture once a week, based on the particular weekly Torah reading. His lecture is directed not only toward clarifying the subject matter but also to the elucidation of textual analysis. In addition, senior *kolel* students will occasionally deliver lectures to one of the *haburot*.

One other unique aspect of the Ner Israel Kolel is the introduction of the *haburah* method as early as high school. *Kolel* students gain practical experience in secondary education by being appointed leaders of these "seminars" and lecturing to the young students. Indeed, this is a formal requirement of the fellow's course of study and will be of value should he choose a career in Jewish education.[45]

The student may pursue a course of study leading to rabbinic ordination, though this is a function of the *yeshivah* rather than the *kolel* per se. Aside from a specialized curriculum, this requires an extensive oral examination administered by the *rosh yeshivah* together with other members of the faculty.

Ner Israel holds the distinction of having authorization to grant the degrees of Bachelor, Master, and Doctor of Talmudic Law. This requires a second curricular track with its own unique requirements. Thus, the candidate for a Master of Talmudic Law must

> . . . choose a field of special study in some department of Talmudic Law . . .
> . . . pursue his graduate work in residence at this college for two full academic years . . .
> . . . prepare a thesis on a subject within his approved field of study . . .
> . . . defend his thesis at an examination to be given in the presence of at least three members of the faculty . . .[46]

A comprehensive written examination may be added at the discretion of the faculty.

Faculty

The faculty and staff of the *kolel* and of the *yeshivah* are virtually identical. The *rosh yeshivah* and the instructors share their responsibilities at both levels, and it is difficult to distinguish between the two. With the exception of R. Ruderman himself, all faculty members are graduates of Ner Israel. Thus, inbreeding with regard to personnel results in virtual conformity in terms of ideology and educational method.

The *kolel* does have its own executive director who is charged with administrative and financial matters, although his secretarial staff is shared with the *yeshivah*, as are custodial and kitchen personnel. Faculty members are housed on the campus of the institution and are provided with medical benefits. Their annual salary is $20,000, and their functions are almost exclusively academic, with little fund-raising or promotional work required.[47]

Students

The students of the Ner Israel Kolel reflect a substantial blend of both Jewish and secular culture, within the confines that *kolel* life requires. The overwhelming majority are American-born, between the ages of 23 and 32. About half hold university degrees, and some intend to pursue postgraduate degrees upon graduation from the *kolel*. Equally, about 20 percent are the sons of rabbis and half have relatives who themselves attended a *kolel*.

The cultural mix is a result of the *yeshivah* policy that permits one to pursue an undergraduate degree at neighboring universities. A student exercising this option may receive a substantial number of credits for his *yeshivah* study. Such a program, practiced by several other institutions under discussion in this study, is an important means of attracting students who might not otherwise attend a *kolel* or for whom a *kolel* might be overly confining and restrictive.

Ner Israel has had particular success in attracting several foreign students, notably Iranians who have come to the United States in increasing numbers in recent years. Special religious services have been organized for this group, and social functions have been introduced to ease their entry.[48]

The family life of *kolel* students appears fairly typical of others under discussion. Many have three or more children who attend local elementary *yeshivot*. Virtually all wives must work outside the home to supplement family income. They work as teachers, secretaries, or librarians. The families socialize and appear to get along well, with minor complaints about child care and the like. The presence of these families in and around the *yeshivah* serves as an important model for younger students, who frequently come in contact with *kolel* fellows as lecturers, tutors, and counselors.

Although the social environment of these families is fairly relaxed and secure, some concern is expressed about job opportunities upon graduation. The *yeshivah* prides itself on the quality of practicing rabbis and teachers it has produced and projects these graduates in various publications and listings. It also encourages students and alumni to produce scholarly and academic publications, and lists these in its promotional literature. To this end, the *yeshivah* publishes its own journal, *Kuntres Or HaKolel*, which contains articles and notes by students, alumni, and faculty.[49]

Nevertheless, there is no formal career guidance for present students beyond the personal contact with a particular faculty member. For those who intend to pursue a career outside Jewish education or communal service, this may be just as well. For those who are interested in Jewish life as a vocation, this is a weakness and has produced some uncertainty and discomfort among several *kolel* families.[50]

The general atmosphere of the Ner Israel Kolel appears relaxed, though a clear and particular goal is pursued with intensity. This constructive spirit of unity and mutual identification can be ascribed to two factors. Physically, the institution has its own campus in a suburban setting which provides housing for many students and faculty. The isolation from external influence, and the rustic surroundings, tend to promote introspection, concentration on study, and a sense of empathy with other members of the *yeshivah* community.

The more important influence, however, is the personality and dynamic magnetism of the *rosh yeshivah*, R. Ruderman, who founded the institution and still takes great personal pride in its accomplishments and particularly in its students. The following comment from a *kolel* fellow is illustrative:

> His [Ruderman's] modesty, demeanor, love for his students set the pace for all of us. He is very respectful of each one of us and so we are respectful of each other. There is a spirit of vitality that he has projected so we want to do our share to improve the Jewish community. What a privilege it is to walk across campus from his home to the *Bais Medrash* [study hall].[51]

In tune with this expression of respect, admiration, and the desire to promote Jewish values, Ner Israel has undertaken an extensive program of community outreach and continuing adult education. This has taken two forms: (a) a daily program for the Orthodox community of Baltimore and its environs and (b) a more formalized course of study for those outside the Orthodox community.

For the Orthodox community, regular lectures are delivered in neighboring areas, throughout the week. *Kolel* students lead classes in Talmudic texts, contemporary *halakhic* problems, and *Mishnah Berurah*. The *yeshivah* claims some 400 regular participants in these classes, many of whom are alumni of Ner Israel who have been attracted to the area precisely because of such services and programs. Thus, an important symbiotic relationship has developed that makes the local community more appealing and provides future students and supporters for the *yeshivah*.

For those outside the Orthodox community, the *yeshivah* has created the Eitz Haim Center for Jewish Studies. This basic and introductory program emphasizes ethics, philosophy, holiday ritual, and some Talmud on a topical basis over the course of the semester. The audience consists largely of young professionals and students at local universities, many of whom have little or no Jewish background and are largely ignorant of Jewish observance. The *yeshivah* claims to have influenced hundreds of these participants to accept Jewish practice and many have joined the *kolel* community as spouses, parents, and supporters of the institution.

The success of these outreach programs is evident in the appointment of a *kolel* graduate as full-time director of adult education. Institutions elsewhere have consulted with Ner Israel in developing similar study centers, and Ner Israel students work with public school children and youth groups throughout the community. There is little doubt that outreach has become an important part of the mission and mandate of this institution.[52]

The activities of the *kolel* include its alumni as well, and there is concerted effort to maintain contact. The *kolel* publishes a bimonthly alumni bulletin with listings of the activities and accomplishments of its graduates, particularly as these relate to their support for the alma mater. The institution sponsors an annual *melave malkah* (festive meal held on a Saturday night) for purposes of homecoming and fund raising.

To serve the needs of its graduates, the *kolel* offers programs for its alumni. Those who have remained in the Baltimore area may take part in classes and lectures held in the Park Heights community, not far from the *yeshivah*. An annual *yarhei kallah* program brings graduates from all parts of the country back to the campus for an extended period of intensive study, usually during summer months when regular sessions are suspended. In addition, the *rosh yeshivah* and other faculty members periodically travel to New York to deliver lectures for graduates residing in that area.

Accountability

Accountability of students at the Ner Israel Kolel is rather loosely defined. The institution is small (fifty students), and it is, therefore, possible for the faculty and the *mashgi'ah* to maintain personal contact with students and monitor their individual progress. However, it should be recalled that faculty members also have important responsibilities within the *yeshivah*, and their contact with *kolel* fellows is consequently limited.

Attendance and punctuality are regularly monitored, and the institution takes these matters seriously. There is, however, no formal system for penalizing students for poor attendance, nor are there any other formal incentives to increase performance and progress. Fellows study independently within the context of the *hevrutah* or *haburah*, and it is asserted that the student's success can be directly observed by the faculty and the *mashgi'ah*.

Only those students who pursue one of the formal degree programs are monitored carefully, and they are subject to a rigid course of study; formal examinations and a written dissertation are required. There is no indication, however, that the academic rigor that characterizes the graduate school of the *yeshivah* exercises any appreciable influence over the *kolel*, its students, faculty, or curriculum.

4. GUR ARYEH INSTITUTE FOR ADVANCED JEWISH SCHOLARSHIP—MESIVTA CHAIM BERLIN

The Yeshiva Rabbi Chaim Berlin represents one of the first institutions to offer traditional Jewish learning in the United States. Organized as Tifferet Bahurim in 1906, it began as a program of afternoon studies for young boys in the Brownsville section of Brooklyn, then a thriving community of immigrant Jewish families. The school was renamed in 1912 as a memorial to Rabbi Chaim Berlin, a leading European rabbi who died that year. A permanent residence was purchased for the institution in the mid-1920s. By 1933, it is estimated that over 400 students were enrolled in its elementary school program.[53]

In 1935 the institution incorporated a high school program and added a rabbinical program in 1936. The year 1939 constituted a turning point in the development of the institution with the appointment of R. Isaac Hutner (1907–1981) as *rosh yeshivah*, under whose influence Yeshiva Chaim Berlin became a high-ranking institution. R. Hutner reorganized the *yeshivah* along the lines of its European counterparts and introduced the systematic study of Talmud, Jewish law, and *musar*. The *yeshivah* was profoundly marked by the personality and leadership of its *rosh yeshivah* for the forty-two years of his administration.

R. Hutner was born in Warsaw and studied at the Yeshiva of Slabodka. He later attended a branch of that institution in Hebron, Israel, where he remained until the Arab massacre of 1929 that led to the disappearance of the Jewish community from that city. He returned to Europe, studied philosophy at the University of Berlin, and undertook independent research in several areas of Talmud and rabbinic thought.[54]

R. Hutner arrived in America in 1935 and served briefly on the faculty of the Rabbi Jacob Joseph Yeshiva until his call to the position of *rosh yeshivah* at Chaim Berlin. From the beginning, he established close and intimate relationships with each of his students, calling them by first names and instilling in them a great sense of pride in their *yeshivah* and their studies. R. Hutner was a powerful and energetic rabbi, qualities which enabled him to hold sway over community leaders and school board members.

The effects of his influence were profound. In the words of one researcher:

> R. Hutner's powerful personality may have been responsible for a certain espirit de corps and in some cases elitism on the part of many students in the *yeshivah* who let it be known to those attending other *yeshivas* that their institution was in a class by itself.[55]

It is telling in this regard that in his later years R. Hutner was referred to as *admor*, a term of respect generally reserved for *hasidic* rabbis by their most ardent followers. Though clearly of Lithuanian training and orientation, his impact upon his students rivaled that of a *hasidic rebbe* in the most tightly woven community. (Whether the epithet "Mother of Yeshivos"—a term Yeshiva Chaim Berlin has arrogated to itself in its official publications—is overly pretentious or well deserved is outside the boundaries of our concerns.)[56]

In 1957, Chaim Berlin added a *kolel*, the Gur Aryeh Institute for Advanced Jewish Scholarship. The name is taken from one of the works by R. Judah Loewe of Prague, whose writings had an important influence upon R. Hutner's thought. It was R. Hutner's design to keep the *kolel* small and elite. Indeed, the institution began with only ten students.[57]

Kolel Structure

The Kolel Gur Aryeh of Yeshiva Chaim Berlin is housed in the *yeshivah* building in the Flatbush-Midwood section of Brooklyn. It includes a large *bet midrash* shared with the entire institution, classrooms, and dining facilities. Its library contains some 10,000 volumes of Talmud, commentaries, and related texts. In 1971 the *kolel* acquired the Yeshiva Bais Hatalmud of Jerusalem, now known as Bais Hatalmud/Gur Aryeh. Though the affiliated *kolel* there is still quite small, plans for a new campus in the Sanhedria section of the city have already been approved.[58]

Applicants to the *kolel* program must be married. The majority of the thirty fellows who studied at the *kolel* in 1982 were graduates of the lower division and were well known to the faculty and administration of the *kolel* upon application. Therefore, no formal examination or admission procedure was required of them.

Those who apply from elsewhere, however, must bring references from their instructors, show evidence of at least four years of *bet midrash* study, and sit for an oral examination. This procedure was administered by R. Hutner until his death in 1981. This duty and other responsibilities have been assumed by R. Aharon Schechter, successor to the position of *rosh yeshivah* and sole admissions officer.

In formal terms, the *kolel* places emphasis upon the applicant's ability to study independently. It seeks those who are familiar with the classical methods of Talmudic research and who are prepared for the "critical examination" of texts and commentaries so as to shed "new light on the organic wholeness of Talmudic knowledge."[59] Yet observation and interview suggest that the process is far less formal and demanding.

Upon admission, students receive a monthly stipend of $375 plus $25 for each child. In addition, bonuses are available based on seniority within the institution. Work-study programs are provided on a limited basis, and *kolel* students receive annual increases.

Though the *kolel* is located in the midst of a residential area with a high concentration of Orthodox and non-Orthodox Jews, it appears that its impact upon the community has been minimal, apart from the influence of the *yeshivah* as a whole.[60] Indeed, the area has reflected an increase in the numbers of observant Jewish families and the services available to them, but it is difficult to assign these changes to the presence of the *kolel* per se. Aside from individual instances, *kolel* fellows have not personally involved themselves with community life.[61]

Program of Study

The Kolel Gur Aryeh has a residency requirement of five years, though students occasionally transfer to other *kolelim* or leave to enter business. In general, however, students remain between five and ten years. In 1982, *kolel* students ranged in age from 24 to 30 years.

The daily schedule of study from Sunday to Thursday begins at 9:15 A.M. and continues until 9:45 P.M. On Fridays the sessions end at 1:30 P.M. Studies are suspended for Jewish holidays, and there are no classes during the month of Av. The *kolel* is transferred to Camp Morris in Woodridge, New York, during the summer months, where cabins and bungalows are available for the students and their families.

The daily program is divided into three *sedarim*: 9:15 A.M. to 1:30 P.M., 3:00 P.M. to 6:45 P.M., and 8:00 P.M. to 9:45 P.M. During the morning *seder* all *kolel* students study the same Talmudic tractate as that chosen for the *yeshivah*. This follows a nine-year annual cycle, and *kolel* fellows may study with their *hevrutah* or with younger *yeshivah* students.[62] The *rosh yeshivah* delivers a lecture every Thursday at 10:00 A.M. and Fridays at 11:30 A.M. Though this is primarily geared towards students of the *bet midrash*, *kolel* students are welcome and do attend regularly.

The last fifteen minutes of the morning *seder* are set aside for the study of *musar*. Such a practice was close to the heart of R. Hutner, and there were recent but unsuccessful attempts to extend this period. Following R. Hutner's passing, the likelihood that these efforts will be renewed in the immediate future appears slim.

During the afternoon session, students work with their *hevrutot*, pursuing areas of individual interest and independent research. The evening session operates similarly except that students in their first year of marriage will generally not return to the *yeshivah* at night.[63]

The pursuit of rabbinic ordination was never a central part of study at the Kolel Gur Aryeh. Consequently, there are no formal degree programs, clearly enunciated requirements, or examinations. This is rationalized as a way of ensuring intellectual creativity within the *kolel* environment. As a matter of course, all graduates of the *kolel* do receive one degree or another as subjectively determined and decided by the *rosh yeshivah*.[64]

Faculty

The faculty of the *kolel* includes two instructors, R. Aharon Schechter and R. Jonathan David, as well as a *mashgi'ah*, R. Shimon Groner. All are are graduates of Yeshiva Chaim Berlin and leading students of the late R. Hutner. R. David is married to R. Hutner's daughter, and all three were hand-picked to serve as his successors. Thus, the institution is assured a powerful sense of stability and continuity, adhering to R. Hutner's particular educational and religious philosophies even after his death.

Though each faculty member supervises the work of *kolel* students and presents lectures to them, the primary responsibilities of the faculty are to the *yeshivah* as a whole. This is considered an advantage in that it provides a sense of unity within the institution and helps to avoid "problematic situations which invariably emerge when two organizational entities interact in an official transaction."[65]

Faculty members earn $20,000 per year and receive some medical and health benefits through a special grant program. There is no retirement plan available, nor do they receive housing supplements.

Students

Students at the Kolel Gur Aryeh are generally American-born graduates of *yeshivah* and *bet midrash* programs. Many are the children or siblings of *kolel* graduates who generally aspire to the same for their own children. Although the institution discourages university study, many *kolel* fellows do attend courses at nearby Brooklyn College, and several have earned degrees. The majority are more exclusively devoted to their religious studies and hope to enter Jewish education as instructors or administrators.[66]

Students at the Gur Aryeh Kolel typically have two or three children. Their wives are graduates of a *yeshivah* high school program for girls, often part of the Beth Jacob School system. These women generally work outside the home as teachers, secretaries, typists, and, more recently, computer programmers. They appear satisfied and idealistic about their contribution to their husbands' academic efforts, though some ambivalence has lately been raised regarding the possible neglect of children, owing to the mothers's vocational pursuits.[67] Nevertheless, these women appear to share the conviction that affiliation with the *kolel* has strengthened the relationship between husband and wife and reinforced the foundation for future marital success.

There is little direction for *kolel* students regarding goals or job placement. The administration speaks of its desire to create "responsible scholars," and it is assumed that many graduates will enter the fields of education and communal work. However, there are no formal training programs, student-teacher opportunities, or placement services. Thus, the student must depend upon his relationship with the *rosh yeshivah* and other informal links to develop his skills and market them elsewhere.

The *kolel* does not sponsor nor does it participate in any formal outreach program. There are no classes led by *kolel* students for members of the neighboring communities, nor does the *kolel* attempt to instruct those who are far from Jewish observance. *Kolel* students are not formally involved with any of the local primary or secondary schools, nor do they participate in youth programs, summer camp activities, and the like. In this regard, Chaim Berlin is unlike most of the other subjects of this study.

Nevertheless, the institution has produced many leading educators, administrators, and rabbis who have become involved in various communal and academic institutions throughout the world, and it has thus left its mark upon contemporary Jewish life. This is the given reason for the appellation "yeshiva of 1000 classrooms" that Chaim Berlin adopted for itself, aside from the aforementioned self-identification as the "mother of yeshivos."[68]

The institution points proudly to its alumni who have founded or who now direct institutions of Jewish education in the New York metropolitan region, Memphis, Denver, Baltimore, Pittsburgh, and in its Jerusalem branch. Indeed, the record is impressive and stands as a tribute to the *yeshivah* despite its apparent lack of outreach or placement programs.

The atmosphere within the *kolel* itself is not unlike that of the *yeshivah* broadly. It is vibrant and active, and fosters a strong sense of unity between student and faculty. Despite the passing of R. Hutner, his personality, the warmth he encouraged among his students, and the spirit that he nurtured are still important marks of the institution. To assure continuity, the *yeshivah* has now organized an elementary program specifically for children of its graduates, which has an enrollment of over 500.[69]

The alumni of the *kolel* are closely knit and form a special section within the *yeshivah* alumni network. Their allegiance to the institution is quite impressive, and they participate in various fund-raising programs, dinners, journals, and other activities. The *yeshivah* claims 1,600 graduates who serve in "Torah leadership positions throughout the world."[70]

In addition, there is a sporadic publication program in which alumni, students, and faculty participate. From 1964 to 1981, a six-volume series of *halakhic*, Talmudic, and homiletic essays by R. Hutner was published under the title *Pahad Yizhak*. In addition, the work of students has been featured in earlier publications, such as the Talmudic journals *Maisharim* and *Ihud Talmidei Gur Aryeh*.

Many alumni have undertaken their own scholarly publications, though not in any formal sense, under the sponsorship of the institution. They retain a link with the *yeshivah* by visiting the *bet midrash* for private study and by arranging *hevrutah* groups with others in the area. Consequently, numerous *kolel* graduates have remained in the immediate vicinity, continue to pray at the *yeshivah* on Shabbat and holidays, and maintain regular relations with its faculty and staff.

Accountability

The progress of the *kolel* fellows is measured by subjective standards. The *rosh yeshivah* claims to know each member intimately and claims to develop standards for each individual. Though it is easy to criticize such a procedure, the results are nevertheless quite impressive. The small size of the *kolel*, of course, lends itself to such informality, and the emphasis on individual standards is said to compensate for the lack of written or oral tests that would give us objective criteria.

5. KOLEL NER DAVID OF YESHIVAT RABBI-ISRAEL MEIR HAKOHEN RABBINICAL SEMINARY OF AMERICA

Yeshivat Rabbi Israel Meir Hakohen is named for the scholar and sage who was popularly known as the *Hafez Hayyim* of Radun (1838–1933). He was the author of such popular works as the *Mishnah Berurah*, a commentary on the *Shulhan Arukh*; *Orah Hayyim*; and *Sefer Shmirat Halashon*, dealing with laws concerning gossip and slander.[71] The *yeshivah* was established by his nephew, R. Dovid Leibowitz (1890–1942), who hoped to perpetuate the synthesis of Talmudic and ethical studies that characterized the *Hafez Hayyim*. R. Leibowitz was also a student at the *yeshivah* of Slobodka and was deeply influenced by its merger of Talmudic study with *musar*.[72]

R. Leibowitz arrived in the United States in 1926 on a fund-raising mission for the *kolel* of Slobodka. He was prevailed upon by R. Shraga Feival Mendlowitz, then director of Mesivta Torah Vodaath, to become head of the newly formed *bet midrash* in an attempt to raise the prestige and status of that institution. R. Leibowitz accepted the position on the recommendation of his renowned uncle, although there appear to have been conflicts and ambivalence in his move from the outset.

R. Leibowitz brought with him the traditions of Lithuania, whose program of Talmudic study and *musar* training was constructed for the full-time *yeshivah* student. But R. Mendlowitz envisioned an institution that would also fulfill the needs of the educated layman and offer study in Jewish history, philosophy, and *hasidic* culture. Questions of personality and temperament were also involved, and R. Leibowitz left Torah Vodaath to found his own *yeshivah* in 1933.[73]

The avowed goal of the new institution was to "duplicate the scholarship, philosophy and atmosphere of Slobodka" and to equip individuals "to meet the leadership needs of the contemporary Jewish community."[74] To that end, the *yeshivah* established the Ner David Rabbinical Graduate Institute (also known as the Ner David Kolel) in the early 1940s as a tribute to its founder, who had died in 1942. The *kolel* was led by R. Henoch Leibowitz, the *rosh yeshivah*, son and successor to R. Dovid Leibowitz. It claims to be the first of its kind in the United States.[75]

Kolel Structure

The Yeshivat Rabbi Israel Meir Ha-Kohen is housed in a three-story building in Forest Hills, a residential section of Queens, New York. The *kolel* occupies a small *bet midrash* and several small, adjacent classrooms. In 1982 there were 38 students in the *kolel*. The *yeshivah* provides a general library and a special reference library with some 2,000 volumes each, and these are for the use of all students within the institution. There are no research facilities specifically for *kolel* fellows. There are also kitchen and dining facilities as well as administrative offices, though again these service the entire *yeshivah*.

This close linkage between the *kolel* and other units of the *yeshivah* is evident in organizational and curricular terms as well. The institution considers its *bet midrash* as the first tier of its graduate program, and indeed most *kolel* students are its graduates. A candidate for admission to the *kolel* must complete at least three-and-a-half years in the *bet midrash* and must pass a series of oral examinations prior to admission. This implies mastery of some 500 pages of Talmud and related literature. In addition, the candidate must submit letters of reference from the faculty. Applicants from other institutions will also sit for an oral examination administered by the *rosh yeshivah* and *mashgi' ah*.[76]

Unlike most other institutions, marriage is not a requirement for acceptance in Kolel Ner David and ten of its students in 1982 were not married. Fellows of the *kolel* range in age from 22 to 35 years.[77]

Upon acceptance, a new kolel student receives a stipend of $60 per week plus $12.50 per week for each of his first two children. In addition, students may receive small bonuses for participating in *mishmar* sessions (Thursday evening study groups) or delivering lectures to younger students. There are assistantships available as well as government loans, grants, and work-study programs. The *yeshivah* also makes scholarships and short-term interest-free loans available to its students. Nevertheless, finances are problematic for many *kolel* students; those with children have found it necessary to seek part-time employment as a supplement.[78]

Adding to this strain is the fact that the *kolel* does not offer subsidized housing to its students. Since the *kolel* is convenient to mass transit, students can live almost anywhere in the New York metropolitan area. Most appear to remain in the immediate locale and must compete for expensive housing in and around Forest Hills.

Although the presence of the *kolel* has not had a profound influence upon local community life, its students have participated in several programs geared to raise the standards of Jewish life and study within the neighborhoods of their residence. Some offer classes in Talmud, Jewish law, and Bible at local synagogues as well as in individual homes. Though these are generally taught on a voluntary basis, synagogues have occasionally offered a modest honorarium to these fellows.

In addition, *kolel* students were instrumental in developing the *Hevra Kaddishah* (burial society) of Queens. They lead classes at a local girls' *yeshivah* and tutor eighth graders from a second school. They have also participated in the Jewish Education Program of Agudath Israel in the hope of encouraging public-school and *yeshivah* students to increase their study of Jewish culture through clubs, seminars, and summer camp programs.[79]

Fellows of Kolel Ner David normally spend three to six years within the institution, depending upon personal, familial, and economic circumstances. Curricular emphasis is placed upon Talmud and Jewish law, with special focus upon "practical personality development."[80] *Kolel* students attend lectures delivered by the *rosh yeshivah* and three *mashgihim* (counselors), and are required to lead classes and study sessions for younger students within the *yeshivah*.

In addition, the *kolel* has introduced a *bahelfer* (facilitator) program to promote interaction between its fellows and the younger students. Designated fellows study with and counsel individual students or groups to help them organize and manage their programs and to encourage independent research.[81] Those who have served as *bahelfers* claim that the experience is invaluable in developing necessary skills for teaching, guidance, and administration.[82]

Program of Study

Kolel students attend classes six days each week, with time off for Jewish holidays and a vacation period during the month of Av. Students may be penalized for unexcused absence, and repeated offenses may result in expulsion from the program.

The typical day begins at 9:30 A.M. following morning prayers, and is divided into three sessions. The morning *seder* extends until afternoon prayers and lunch, normally about 2:30 P.M. Here all *kolel* fellows study the same tractate as the *yeshivah* generally so that they can be prepared to lecture and tutor the younger students. The *yeshivah* follows a seven-year cycle and eight tractates are covered.[83]

Following lunch the students of the *kolel* concentrate on various *musar* texts until 4:00 P.M. The third session then extends until 7:30 P.M. Here the fellows are permitted some discretion in their studies of other tractates, as well as texts relating to Jewish law. These generally include selections dealing with holiday service, civil law, and family law.[84]

For purposes of study, each fellow must join a *haburah* of his choice, a process that is supervised and monitored by the administration. In addition, there are weekly seminars with younger students to discuss and analyze various lectures delivered by the *rosh yeshivah*. Each member of the *kolel* is periodically invited to develop and present some piece of independent research before faculty and peers, and thus demonstrate his progress and performance.

Students are not required to pursue rabbinical ordination, though experience indicates that all do. A fellow is expected to complete three years of study before undertaking a prescribed course dealing with Yoreh De'ah and Hoshen Mishpat (ritual and civil law, respectively). The entire process generally takes five years and must be completed within six.[85]

In addition, the *yeshivah* offers special programs geared toward the practical elements of community relations and public speaking. Recognizing that many of its graduates will undertake positions in the rabbinate, community service, and educational administration, the *yeshivah* has called upon leading members of these professions in the New York metropolitan area to lead workshops and classes designed to develop the necessary skills. Though limited, the program appears to be well received by the students.

In methodological terms, the *kolel* is somewhat unique. The emphasis upon the encyclopedic volume of a student's progress is far less than in many other *kolelim* cited in this study. Rather, students focus upon *sugyot* (units of Talmudic discussion) and review them in great depth and detail.

The administration views this as a superior mode of analysis and points to Lithuanian antecedents of this pattern, such as the Yeshivah of Slobodka. Nevertheless, detractors question the wisdom and purpose of such an approach. In the words of one critic:

> Even our greatest commentaries have ended their comments with the remark "this still needs greater elucidation." But, nevertheless, they continue to the next point and do not stop.[86]

Another distinguishing trait of the Ner David Kolel is the means by which it facilitates secular education for its students. Though not encouraged to pursue a university education, students are granted sixty credits for their *yeshivah* study through a special arrangement with the registrar's office at Queens College of the City University of New York. Transcripts are presented from the *yeshivah*, noting formal coursework in Jewish history, philosophy, and Hebrew. This has been an important aspect of the program, allowing students to continue their *kolel* work while securing an advantage in the pursuit of a university degree.[87]

An unusual element of the Ner David Kolel program is its link with a branch institution in Jerusalem. Opened in 1965, this unit is known as

Yeshivat Hafez Hayyim of Jerusalem and is located in Sanhedria Mur-hevet, a new residential area on the outskirts of the city. It is presently directed by R. Moshe Chait, an alumnus of the institution in America and a successful rabbi and teacher in his own right. In 1981, the *yeshivah* insti-tuted a requirement for all candidates to spend a year of study at its Jerusalem branch prior to acceptance in the *kolel*. In 1982, almost all the students had fulfilled that requirement.[88]

Faculty

The faculty of the *kolel* consists of the *rosh yeshivah* and three *mash-gihim*. The former is a noted scholar who lectures periodically, generally in English. The latter are graduates of the Ner David Kolel and serve in an academic and counseling capacity. The faculty salary is roughly $25,000 per year and includes a limited retirement plan but no medical benefits. Faculty are not provided with living accommodations. In addition, the ad-ministration also includes an executive director and secretarial staff, aside from support services available to the *yeshivah* generally.[89]

Students

The overwhelming majority of the students of Kolel Ner David are American-born graduates of the *yeshivah*'s lower division. They are marked by their modern dress and proper deportment, an element that is attributed to the original influence of its founder, R. Dovid Leibowitz. Though most pursue secular studies as noted, they all aspire to excellence in their reli-gious studies and display a willingness to sacrifice to attain their goal.

Their family life varies. Several are single, and others are married but have no children. Generally, students of this institution appear more wil-ling to delay childbirth as compared to those of other *kolelim* under discus-sion here. Their wives are typically graduates of a girls' *yeshivah*, and many have studied in Israel as part of a foreign-student program there.

The women particularly express an appreciation for their husbands' work. They note the great honor of supporting Torah study and take pride in their social and theological role in this project. And one notes, "But even beyond that is the thought that a *Talmid Hakham* [rabbinic scholar] makes a good husband and father. It may not always be so . . . but 99 percent of the time it is."[90]

These women often seek employment outside the home. Some are teachers in local *yeshivot* and Hebrew schools, others do office work in Manhattan. More recently, it has become common for wives of *kolel* students to study computer programming and take advantage of ex-pansions in that field.

The families appear to form close relationships and reside in close proximity to the *yeshivah*. They meet during holidays and vacations and maintain active social relations. Indeed, this has also served as a matchmaking network for unmarried members of the *kolel*.

As regards career aspirations, the *yeshivah* appears to take its mandate as a training ground for professional Jewish leadership most seriously. *Kolel* students are strongly encouraged to pursue careers in the rabbinate and Jewish education, both formally and informally. As noted, the instructional methodology of the institution as well as its activities within the local community enhance these opportunities and the training of students so inclined.

However, the *yeshivah* has not contented itself with local accomplishments alone. Both because of its commitment to traditional Jewish values and its desire to help promote its graduates, the Kolel Ner David and the parent *yeshivah* have undertaken an aggressive outreach program to far-flung Jewish communities throughout the United States, and its graduates have been placed in positions of influence as a result.

The *yeshivah* lists numerous institutions of Jewish learning that have been established by graduates of its central program or that are now directed by its alumni. Aside from those in metropolitan New York, these include schools located in Rochester and Buffalo, New York; Phoenix and Tucson, Arizona; Los Angeles, California; New Haven, Connecticut; and Dallas, Texas.

The *kolel* itself is bathed in an atmosphere of intense and serious study. Classes are interspersed with lively debate and vigorous analysis, yet never beyond the bounds of fellowship and cordiality. According to many alumni, the result is a sense of challenge and achievement.[91]

The goals and aspirations of the *kolel* administration are still very much marked by the personality of its founder. There is a sense of mission among the students and dedication toward reaching the broader Jewish community. The students seem secure and, despite some financial hardships, show no apparent strain.

This general aura of well-being is also attributable to the personality and administrative style of the present director, R. Henoch Leibowitz. Students and alumni consult regularly with him. There is a fatherly demeanor in his relationship with the students, and his home is open to them. The men of the *kolel* respond accordingly. He and his wife frequently host Friday evening dinners for various groups of students and welcome individuals on the Sabbath day for discussions of personal affairs and counseling. They are personally involved in the family lives of their students and have often helped to bring about financial arrangements with parents and relatives.[92]

Finally, the *yeshivah* has undertaken interesting off-time programs to foster loyalty and solidarity among its students. For some years the entire student body was moved to a Catskill Mountain retreat for summer study sessions.[93] In addition, every third year the *rosh yeshivah* visits the Jerusalem branch in order to deter any sense of isolation and alienation among those students, many of whom will enter *kolel* life soon thereafter.

Unlike many other institutions under discussion, this *kolel* does not produce a journal or a review to showcase the scholarship of its fellows and alumni. No alumni organization has emerged, though the *kolel* claims over 100 graduates. Nevertheless, the group does continue to maintain close relations with its alma mater, supporting it financially and contributing to its various fund-raising drives.

Interviews with alumni are revealing. All speak warmly about their years in the *kolel*. Their sole criticism concerns the insufficient training in human relations and guidance, and a desire for more intensive training in matters of practical Jewish law.

Wives of alumni reflect much the same opinion. Their years of affiliation with the *kolel* were satisfying though often accomplished at the expense of material comfort and financial gain. They would urge their children to pursue the same goals and often set *kolel* study as a prenuptial requirement during their children's first years of marriage.[94]

As a group, most alumni are university graduates. Many maintain high levels of community activity, even if they have not entered Jewish education or the rabbinate. As a further tribute to the impact of their *kolel* years, alumni claim a continued link with Talmudic study, some allegedly devoting forty hours per week to these pursuits. Admittedly, such intensity is generally limited to those whose study is linked to their professions.

Although he focuses on the *yeshivah* in general, Helmreich does offer several comments that may be extended to the Ner David Kolel. For example, he speaks of the existence of a "Hafez Hayyim Yeshiva" type:

> He is a person dedicated to Jewish education, willing to reach out beyond his community and careful in his ethical and moral conduct.[95]

He speaks of

> esprit de corps and charismatic leadership both of which are, in some measure, responsible for making *Chofetz Chaim* [sic] one of the more successful *yeshivas* in the country.[96]

The unique aspects of Kolel Ner David are reflected in its program of study, its relationship with university education, its link to the State of

Israel, and its perceptions of the broader Jewish community. These variables undoubtedly influence the quality of its graduates as compared with those of other such institutions. Comparisons of this nature are comprehensively discussed in a later chapter.

Accountability

Accountability at Kolel Ner David is unsystematic, though somewhat more formal than elsewhere. There are no written examinations or grades, and no preparation or defense of independent research is required before graduation. As noted, attendance is monitored carefully, and students receive incentives for their participation in a given academic or communal program.

Several informal elements are noteworthy. Though not required, virtually all students do pursue rabbinic ordination. Thus, a structured curriculum is maintained, and obtaining the degree is contingent upon passing an oral examination before the faculty. Since most fellows are graduates of the *bet midrash*, their abilities and their potential are well known to the faculty, and this tends to promote an inherent sense of responsibility for one's progress.

Furthermore, the institution is small, extremely close-knit, and highly reflective of the personality and leadership of the *rosh yeshivah*. R. Leibowitz and his three *mashgihim* devote time and effort to maintain a warm but nonetheless firm and clear perspective on each student. As noted elsewhere, accountability is a subjective process, closely related to matters of individual taste and need, and to the personalities of the students involved. Ner David, however, is a more successful example of such a system than other *kolelim* in this study.

6. KOLEL AVREICHIM CHABAD LUBAVITCH

The Chabad-Lubavitch Movement was founded by R. Schneur Zalman of Liadi (1745–1813), an early *hasidic* leader. The term "Chabad" is an acronym for *hokhmah, binah,* and *daat* (wisdom, understanding, and knowledge). It was R. Schneur's intent to integrate the great spiritual emotionalism of *hasidic* philosophy with serious intellectual endeavor, an undertaking unique for its time and one that has left its stamp upon the movement to this day.[97]

R. Dovber, son of R. Schneur Zalman, settled in the White Russian town of Lubavitch in 1814. This became the central residence of the

Chabad movement until 1916, when World War I and the Russian Revolution caused it to seek asylum elsewhere. Under Stalinist persecutions, Chabad was forced to move to Riga in 1928. In 1934 it moved once more to Warsaw, and in 1940 the central organization and its various institutions took up residence in the United States.[98]

During the early period the leaders of Chabad assumed the surname Schneerson and produced numerous works of responsa and Talmudic analysis. In addition, a complex, three-tiered educational system was developed in several neighboring towns, sponsored in large measure by the movement's central organization and subsidized by local leadership. These *yeshivot* were known as *hadarim*—a term usually reserved for early childhood education—and admitted both single and married students.[99]

In an attempt to open Torah study to a larger and younger constituency, the Yeshiva Tomchei T'mimim was established in the town of Lubavitch in 1897 under the sponsorship of the fifth *rebbe*, R. Sholom Dovber, who appointed his son, R. Joseph Isaac, as its principal. The aim was to counter the influence of the *haskalah*, the Jewish Enlightenment that called for the integration of secular culture in Jewish life and thought. It should be noted that the period was a propitious one for the founding of *yeshivot*, and Tomchei T'mimim was only one of several illustrious *yeshivot* established, among them Slobodka, Mir, Slutsk, and Telz.

But the Chabad institution was to be somewhat different. There was a fundamental commitment to the study of Torah, Talmud, and the Jewish classics, but Tomchei T'mimim would also include an intensive study of *hasidic* texts. It would foster a vision of its students as "militants for Torah" and unite them to each other and to the *rebbe* as their leader.[100]

The result was a unique admixture that is still reflected in Lubavitch institutions today. From these institutions there emerged a student who was devoutly pious in his religious observance, but who was also concerned with the physical and spiritual needs of the outside world. He was firmly committed to his Talmudic studies but integrated them with the mystical and spiritual elements of *hasidism*.[101]

R. Joseph Isaac succeeded his father as *rebbe* in 1920 and presided over the movement's transfer to Riga, Warsaw, and to Brooklyn in 1940. He was joined by his son-in-law, R. Menaham M. Schneerson, who acceded to the position upon the former's death in 1950. Under the present *rebbe*, Chabad has undertaken a major expansionist philosophy in the hope of bringing Jewish culture to far-flung communities throughout the world and to Jews who are quite distant from the tradition.

The Kolel of Chabad—officially known as the Kolel Avreichim Al Yad Mazkirus Kvod Kedushat Admor-Shalita—was founded by R. Menahem

M. Schneerson in 1960. Its avowed aim was to create a training ground for future Jewish leadership and particularly for the dynamic brand of outreach promoted and developed by Chabad. The *kolel* is an extension of the central Yeshiva Tomchei T'mimim in America and thus is bound to "follow the school of religious belief known as Lubavitz or Chabad and shall at all times be under the supervision of the Lubavitcher Rabbi of each generation."[102]

Kolel Structure

The Chabad Kolel is located near the movement's headquarters in the Crown Heights section of Brooklyn, an area once known for its large Orthodox Jewish community; at present, it is an ethnically and racially mixed neighborhood. Indeed, the Chabad community constitutes the bulk of the current Jewish population in Crown Heights. The *kolel* has its own study hall and library, and most students live in the immediate area.

The *kolel* library has some 2,000 volumes and an additional 1,000 volumes located at the *yeshivah*'s central library nearby. *Kolel* students also have access to the *Rebbe*'s personal library, which is reputed to house over 50,000 volumes, including rare books and manuscripts and one of the world's most extensive collections of Jewish mystical and *hasidic* works. The *yeshivah* also maintains a collection of audio and video tapes of the *Rebbe*'s lectures and various gatherings of the movement.

The express purpose of the *kolel* is to promote Jewish scholarship and the dissemination of Chabad and *hasidic* philosophy. Students are expected to prepare themselves for an active role in the Chabad community, which may well include special assignment in various parts of the world. In this regard, the institution is unique among those being studied here.[103]

The basis for admission to the *kolel* is somewhat vague. All applicants must be married, and the substantial majority have completed undergraduate programs affiliated with Chabad in Brooklyn or elsewhere in its chain of institutions. In this regard, Chabad is not unlike other *kolelim*. Of course, applicants from similar institutions outside Chabad are considered.

Applicants sit for an oral examination administered by a member of the faculty and are expected to demonstrate their ability to do original research in advanced Talmudic or *halakhic* scholarship.[104] In addition,

> since the students participate in the many Torah programs projected by the *Rebbe*, their ability has already been gauged by their peers and members of the administrative staff and particularly, the *Rebbe*. Similarly, those who

apply from other Chabad institutions throughout the world have been involved in writing, learning and doing. References are readily available.[105]

Upon acceptance, *kolel* students are given a stipend of $220 per month and holiday bonuses of $350. Wives generally work outside the home, frequently as elementary school teachers, and parents or in-laws often supplement the family income. Housing is not provided, and *kolel* families must find accommodations in the immediate area, because the *Rebbe* has forbidden his adherents to leave Crown Heights. Students are eligible for various government housing subsidies and other income-maintenance programs.[106]

Although details of the movement's active outreach program and the specific involvement of *kolel* students within it are presented below, a few words regarding community influence are in order. It should be noted that Chabad was established in Crown Heights at the very birth of its Jewish development in America and soon found itself in the midst of a thriving and affluent Jewish community. However, as a result of the general exodus of middle-class whites from many parts of New York City during the 1960s, Crown Heights very quickly lost the bulk of its Jewish population .

Viewed in this context, the *Rebbe*'s demand that his adherents remain in the area is most significant, in that Chabad constitutes virtually all that is left of Jewish life there. His commitment to maintaining this racially mixed community is exceptional and initially led to conflicts with others who preferred to leave.

On an individual level, *kolel* students take an active part in community life around the institution and in nearby Jewish communities. Adult education classes, special seminars for women, lectures at various synagogues in other parts of the metropolitan area, and youth work are all part of their regular activities. *Kolel* students also man mobile units known as "Mitzvah Tanks," which bring Jewish ritual and practice to heavily traveled thoroughfares in all parts of New York City, and their activities are readily recognizable, particularly as Jewish holidays approach. They serve on a speaker's bureau and have made presentations before various community and youth groups regarding *hasidic* philosophy and their own particular brand of Jewish life.

Program of Study

Students at the Chabad Kolel attend sessions from 8:00 A.M. until 7:00 P.M. six days per week, twelve months per year, with time off only for Jewish holidays. Attendance is monitored very carefully, and the administration claims to be severe regarding punctuality and absence. Yet no formal penalties or systematic incentives appear to exist.

As with other subjects of this study, the daily program is divided into three uneven blocks. From 8:00 A.M. to 9:00 A.M., fellows study *hasidic* thought, notably the works of seven generations of Lubavitcher *rebbes*. Morning prayers and breakfast follow until 11:00 A.M.

Students then work individually and in groups, researching and analyzing the particular Talmudic tractates and selections being covered by the *yeshivah* as a whole. The session adjourns at 2:15 P.M. for afternoon prayers and lunch and resumes at 3:30 P.M. At this point the *hevrutot* reassemble to study topics chosen by the *rosh hakolel*. Many are subjects of practical importance, and the fellows review the sources, rulings, and contemporary applications in turn. Subjects are generally chosen from the Talmudic tractates Zevahim, Menahot, Eruvin, Mikvaot, and Niddah.

The *rosh hakolel* lectures on Tuesday and Thursday afternoons, and guest lecturers are occasionally invited to make presentations regarding some area of Jewish law. Although there is no formal evening session, students are expected to study at home or involve themselves in one or another of the movement's *mitzvah* projects. Overall, the curriculum and the means by which it is presented are oriented toward preparing the student for his mission or assignment upon graduation.[107] Study without practical fulfillment is not considered proper for these students.

There is considerable emphasis upon individual research. Students are expected to prepare presentations for the entire *kolel*, though there does not seem to be any formal program for doing so. Prior to their acceptance in the *kolel*, a number of fellows had already completed a professional program leading to ordination. Open to students who have completed a four-year undergraduate program in the *yeshivah*, this program allows students to pursue a two-year curriculum leading to the traditional rabbinic degree of *Yoreh Yoreh*, the ordination degree conferred for expertise in ritual law.

These fellows are, therefore, encouraged to pursue advanced research in Jewish civil and family law. They have also become heavily involved in several publication projects sponsored by the institution as a whole. Thus far they have published an encyclopedia of *hasidic* philosophy based on the works of the third *Rebbe* of Chabad; manuscripts of the founder of the movement; and the lectures and discourses of the present *Rebbe*. In addition, the movement produces numerous English-language works of scholarly and popular interest in which some of these students have been actively involved.[108]

Faculty

As might be expected in a movement of this kind, the *kolel* is administratively linked not only to the *yeshivah* but also to various other organs of this vast international movement. The *Rebbe* exercises final control over all constituent bodies. He appoints a *rosh yeshivah* who must certify all rabbinic degrees granted by the institution and who works closely with the *hanhalah*, the administrative or educational committee. This body recruits the *rosh hakolel* and provides a *menahel*, principal or administrator, for that unit. Although preference for that position is generally given to members of the Chabad community, faculty positions have been offered to outstanding scholars from without. The present *rosh hakolel* is a graduate of the Lubavitcher Yeshiva in Jerusalem.[109]

His salary is approximately $11,000 per year, and he is provided with health and medical benefits. No pension plan is provided, and appointment ensures lifetime tenure. In the event that a faculty member is forced to retire because of poor health, severance and financial subsidy have been arranged by the institution.[110]

Students

In 1982, there were fifty students at the Chabad-Lubavitch Kolel. An unwritten presumption of attendance is the implicit commitment and dedication to Chabad *hasidism* and its philosophy of international outreach. The majority of the students were American-born graduates of the lower divisions of the *yeshivah*. About twenty, however, came from a variety of foreign countries. Most of these had also studied at a Chabad institution and had proven themselves loyal to the movement.

The typical *kolel* family is newly married and most will have a child before the fellow's graduation. All *kolel* students have chosen women of the Lubavitcher community as their wives. These women are generally involved in various communal activities and see their husbands' vocation as an integral part of their relationship. Indeed, many claim that the husband's study has had a most positive impact on their marriage and was part of a prenuptial agreement, as is the case for other *kolelim* cited in this work.[111]

Much of the social life of these families revolves about a specific aspect of Chabad communal activity: the *farbrenge*. The *farbrenge* is a vast assemblage of the Chabad faithful—students, disciples, sympathizers, or the merely interested—which is held at least once each month. On such occasions the *Rebbe* discourses on some topic of Talmudic, Biblical, or homiletic interest, often speaking for several hours at a time. It is an important event that brings thousands of the community's members into contact with each other and allows them to feel that they are an integral part of the *Rebbe*'s grand scheme.

These gatherings are followed by lively discussions among students regarding some point of the *Rebbe*'s discourse. A select group will be charged with preparing a transcript of the talk, which becomes the text for still more discussion and debate among students. The *yeshivah* sees this process as "a powerful medium for broadening the students' mind," giving them

> close familiarity with numerous subjects not always within the scope of normal *Yeshivah* courses. It affords them frequent glimpses into the unfathomable depth of profundity of one of the great giants of Jewish scholarship in our generation.[112]

As such, the *farbrenge* must be considered a crucial aspect of both the educational and social experience of all *kolel* families.

It is clear that the students of the Chabad Kolel and their families are but a small part of a much larger and close-knit whole. They express their total loyalty and commitment to the movement and its various projects. Indeed, it is interesting that despite (and perhaps because of) this commitment, they are willing to leave the sheltered comfort of their community and eagerly anticipate the assignment that the *Rebbe* and his associates will choose for them. For many, this may mean a mission to some lonely and isolated part of the world. This contrast is reflected in a *kolel* wife's comment:

> Although our marriage was our own choice, my husband's family and mine knew each other for decades. . . . In school the girls always talked about the future and wondered where we would be—in Africa, South America, on some college campus—and how far we would be from our families. There was never any question about wanting to be married to a Lubavitcher and bringing up a family dedicated to Chabad. . . . Maybe that's why there is so little divorce—we know what we want.[113]

The overwhelming majority of *kolel* graduates enter the fields of Jewish education and communal service via the various outreach programs undertaken by the Chabad movement. These programs are the very hallmark of the movement and deserve some elaboration. Lubavitch has centers and missions in almost every state in the country and in twenty-five foreign locations as well. These branch units are intended to bring religious leadership, education, and counseling particularly to *baale teshuvah*, those with little or no Orthodox Jewish background who wish to become observant Jews.

In this regard, Chabad has had considerable success with newly liberated Jews from the Soviet Union and other East European countries, as well as those from Iran and parts of the Arab world. In addition, branches of the Chabad *kolel* have recently been opened in Melbourne, Australia, and in Mexico City.

During the late 1960s, the movement undertook a unique campaign to introduce particular *mitzvot* to those on the periphery of Jewish life. While charity and concern for one's fellow were included in this program, the primary focus was upon ritual commandments that have less universal appeal and visibility. Thus, donning phylacteries during the morning prayers, affixing a *mezuzah*, and observing Jewish dietary restrictions and the laws of *niddah* were among the requirements included in this campaign. *Kolel* students, among others, could be seen at various thoroughfares in all parts of New York City, stopping passersby to influence the Jews among them to consider these rituals, distributing literature, and often handing out ritual objects themselves. The program has continued for some fifteen years and now encompasses ten *mitzvot* as its focus.

The importance of outreach as an element of *kolel* study is clearly reflected in the thinking of the fellows:

> I chose to learn in this *kolel* because of the *Rebbe, Shlita*. I look forward to carry out the mission of bringing Torah and *Hasidus* to the World, as does every *Chabadnik* [follower of Chabad]. I have already spent summers on *shlichus* [assignment] in South America and I know that the discipline imposed upon *kolel yungeleit* [fellows] is important training for the future.[114]

As one might expect, the alumni of the Chabad *kolel* retain strong loyalties toward their alma mater. All have remained within the Chabad movement and articulate their identification less with the *kolel* per se, but rather with the *kolel* as a constituent unit of the entire community.

A formal alumni organization has been established, and regular meetings are held before most *farbrengen*. In addition, there is an annual convention for alumni and their families. Alumni maintain close ties with the *Rebbe* and his associates and actively support the *kolel* financially.

Virtually all alumni send their children to Lubavitcher elementary and secondary schools. Many hold positions of leadership in the various educational, social, and communal organizations sponsored by the movement. Interestingly, because Chabad maintains vigorous programs on many university campuses, some of its graduates come to active Jewish life after having completed their university education, and they later return to campus life as youth workers under the sponsorship of Chabad.

Both students and alumni are involved in an extensive publication program under the auspices of the movement as a whole. The *yeshivah* publishes annual and semi-annual volumes of student essays and alumni papers in the areas of Talmudic research and *hasidic* philosophy, as well as collections of student responsa. Aside from these scholarly efforts, alumni have been involved in the preparation of popular works based on the *Rebbe*'s lectures, and they disseminate literature for use on one or another *mitzvah* campaign or outreach program.

Accountability

As is the case in other *kolelim* cited earlier, accountability within the Chabad *kolel* is difficult to discern and evaluate clearly. But in this case the intense involvement of students at the Chabad *kolel* in the myriad of outreach and communal programs renders the issue of accountability even more problematic.

On the one hand, formal structures do exist whereby student progress might be measured and performance appraised. Attendance records are carefully kept, and students may be penalized financially for unexcused absence or repeated lateness. In addition, reference is made to "comprehensive examinations in the subjects of the Graduate School" and presentation of independent research in "classical philosophical literature . . . and the manuscripts and published works of the seven generations of Chabad leaders," some of which are later published, as noted above.[115]

Yet the point must be made that participation in outreach programs seems to be a major competitive force that could easily distract the student from his primary mission within the *kolel*—uninterrupted study. So many campaigns, programs, projects, and assignments exist that it is hard to see how a fellow could easily give first priority to his studies and simultaneously maintain a high level of sociocommunal activity. Moreover, one of the stated goals of the *kolel* is the preparation of future leaders for precisely such missions, thus incorporating this potential distraction into the curriculum of the institution.

It must be mentioned that *kolel* leaders are sensitive to this possible conflict. They note that all outreach activities are undertaken outside of the *kolel* schedule and are always under the supervision and guidance of Chabad faculty. Students whose academic performance is inadequate will not be permitted to participate in these programs.

Finally, *kolel* fellows must subordinate their communal work to requisite after-hours study. Those who do not give priority to their studies at home are reprimanded by the faculty and may lose their rights to participate in outreach altogether.[116]

7. Kollel Avreikhim of Bobov

The Bobover *hasidic* community traces its beginnings to the end of the nineteenth century, to the small town of Bobov in the Galician region of Poland. Its founder, R. Solomon Halberstam (1847–1906), was scion of a large and illustrious *hasidic* family. His grandfather, R. Hayyim Halberstam, was a prolific author and teacher who founded a *yeshivah*, served as rabbi of Nowy Sacz (Zanz), and studied under R. Jacob Isaac, the "Seer of Lublin."[117]

Solomon settled in Bobov in 1892 and was soon recognized as the Bobover *Rebbe*. He established the Yeshiva Eitz Chaim, which enrolled 300 students within a short time. Other units were founded as the institution grew in popularity; thus, within two decades after his death, branches were established in neighboring regions, which are claimed to have had as many as 7,000 students.[118]

Solomon was succeeded by his son, Ben Zion (1873–1941), in 1906. Under the latter's leadership, the *hasidic* community grew and many were attracted to its institutions. His court was distinguished by its modesty and relative simplicity as well as by the beautiful melodies that were attributed to the *Rebbe*. Sadly, R. Ben Zion Halberstam was among 1,800 Jews who were martyred by the Nazis outside of Lemberg in July 1941.

His son, Solomon, was able to escape the onslaught, however, and found refuge in America in March 1946. The new *Rebbe* settled in the Boro Park section of Brooklyn, attempted to rebuild his community, and founded institutions to replace those that had been lost during the Holocaust. In 1959, Solomon also founded a settlement south of Tel Aviv to be called Bobova, which has attracted many *hasidim* and their families.

In 1971 the Kolel Abvreikhim of Bobov was established under the direction of the present *Rebbe*'s son-in-law, R. Yonasan Goldberger. It began with fifteen students who had been enrolled in the undergraduate unit of the community's *yeshivah*. Though the institution sees itself as a training center for scholars and teachers, this does not appear to have been the primary motivation for its establishment. In the words of its director:

The *hasidic* men normally marry at a young age [ca. 20 years] and it is recognized in the community that they are not prepared to go out into the business world or to enter the professions without first attaining a solid background of Torah knowledge.[119]

This point is explored below.

Kolel Structure

The *kolel* is located in a new building in the Boro Park section of Brooklyn. It has the use of a large *bet midrash* and some 8,000 volumes of Talmudic and related works. There is a dining hall, kitchen facilities, and offices for administrative and academic use. In addition, the building includes a *mikveh* and facilities for baking *matzah* for Passover.

Aside from its Brooklyn center, the *yeshivah* also maintains campuses in the Catskill region of New York for its summer programs. There is a forty-acre camp where the entire student body and much of the administration and faculty are transferred during the months of July and August. In addition, the *kolel* has a separate unit with its own *bet midrash*, and individual cabins are available for each family so that study can continue in a comfortable atmosphere during the summer months, without infringing upon family life.[120]

Admission requirements for the *kolel* include marriage, at least three years of Torah study beyond high school, and demonstrated success in one's studies. Applicants who are graduates of the lower divisions of the Bobover Yeshiva are already well known to the administration and need not be interviewed or examined. Those who apply from elsewhere are required to bring letters of recommendation and to sit for an informal examination administered by the *rosh hakolel*.

Until 1982, all applicants were trained at the undergraduate units of the *yeshivah*. Since then, however, a small percentage of the applicants have come from other institutions—particularly from Monsey, New York, and Lakewood, New Jersey. In May 1982, these numbered 15 of the 90 fellows of the *kolel*. Though not explicitly articulated, it is understood that the applicant will be of *hasidic* background, and his dress, deportment, and behavior must conform to those of the community.

Upon acceptance, students receive no stipends during their first year of attendance. After the first year, fellows are eligible to receive $40 per week plus $20 per week for the first child, and an additional $10 per week for each child thereafter. By these standards alone, there are fellows receiving $100 per week as a basic subsidy. In addition, there are holiday bonuses of up to $200 for those who need them. The student is also encouraged to apply for government rent subsidies, food stamps, medical care, and public assistance programs. The *kolel* provides no housing for its students.

The *kolel* imposes no residency requirement. Most students remain for at least two years, and many commence part-time employment in business or trade soon thereafter. About a third aspire to careers in the rabbinate or education and will, therefore, remain at the *kolel* for an additional five years of research and study. For these, supplemental income is available in the form of part-time employment, tutoring, and remedial work with younger students. Of course, it is not uncommon for *kolel* fellows to be subsidized by parents or in-laws, and many of their wives are employed outside the home.[121]

As a *hasidic* community located in Boro Park, the Bobover group has limited contact with those outside its circle, and most of the interaction is between the disciples of the Bobover *Rebbe*. Consequently, this *kolel*, located in its own communal setting, exerts little influence beyond its own community.

Within this context, *kolel* students lead adult education classes and present lectures that are free and open to the public. It is not unusual for those outside the immediate community to participate in prayers and religious services at the Bobover Yeshiva or to attend a daily Talmud study group, which is occasionally led by one of the *kolel* students. The Bobover community has maintained a generally good rapport with its neighbors and is represented in the Boro Park Council of Jewish Organizations.[122]

Program of Study

The fellows of the Kolel Avreikhim of Bobov study five-and-a-half days each week. From Sunday through Thursday there are two *sedarim* each day, and on Fridays only the morning session is held. Typically, the morning *seder* begins at 9:45 A.M. following morning prayers and breakfast. This continues until 1:30 P.M. Following lunch and afternoon prayers, the second *seder* is held from 3:10 P.M. until 6:45 P.M. The director of the *kolel* lectures every Thursday for one hour. His discourse is followed by a student presentation; the *kolel* fellows lecture on a rotating basis.

There appears to be a great deal of freedom, and this results in some minor controversy about the curriculum of study at the *kolel*. The students are subdivided into *hevrutah* groups. For the morning session in 1981–82, about thirty students chose to review Pesahim, the same Talmudic tractate then being covered by the *yeshivah* collectively. Some thirty-five others joined a special *haburah* with the *rosh hakolel*, and the remainder chose texts of their own preference and worked at their own pace. Except for those studying with the *rosh hakolel*, this autonomy was and is the rule for the afternoon session as well.

The *rosh hakolel* and his *haburah* represent a much more structured approach to study. It has always been R. Goldberger's contention that rather than emphasize texts and the sheer quantity of one's learning, Talmudic sources should be approached from the perspective of *sugyot*. This should be immediately followed by the comprehensive review of later rulings, the *Shulhan Arukh*, and the opinions of modern contemporary scholars.

It appears, however, that the method has not been well received by the students of the *kolel* over the years. Their reluctance may be related to a general desire to allow as much freedom as possible in an establishment much more oriented toward producing educated laymen than senior researchers, scholars, and judges of Jewish law.[123]

Although the study of *hasidic* philosophy is not a formal part of the program, it is implicit in all for which the institution stands. Consequently, fellows generally devote some of their early morning or evening hours to a *hasidic* text, particularly those by the Bobover *Rebbes* and their predecessors.

Efforts are made to offer programs in pedagogy and educational methodology for those who consider education as a career. These are frequently led by guest lecturers who serve as instructors and administrators elsewhere.[124]

The *kolel* confers no degrees nor does it ordain rabbis. In fact, a substantial proportion of the fellows have received their ordination prior to entering and are there to pursue their studies for purely personal satisfaction. Nevertheless, those who do seek ordination can utilize their studies at the *kolel* in preparation for the traditional oral examination, which is then arranged by the *rosh hakolel* in conjunction with prominent local rabbis and authorities. Such students frequently apprentice themselves to these masters prior to undergoing the examination itself.[125]

Faculty

There are two faculty members attached to the Bobover Kolel: the *rosh hakolel* and the *mashgi'ah*. The former reports directly to the Bobover *Rebbe*, who holds the title of President of the Bobover Yeshiva Rabbinical College and is also the *rosh hakolel*'s father-in-law. Aside from his academic and administrative responsibilities, the *rosh hakolel* also serves as a placement officer, seeking out positions for graduates in various local *yeshivot* and educational institutions. (Some thirty graduates had been placed between 1978 and 1982.) For their services, faculty members are paid $250 per week, with no fringe benefits. In addition to the faculty, the *kolel* also has an executive director, an admissions office, kitchen staff, and various maintenance workers.[126]

Students

The overwhelming majority of the students at the Bobover Kolel are American-born members of the Bobover community. They impressed this author as being articulate and sensitive men with a feeling for history and the place of the Bobover *hasidic* community therein. The elder students have large families, and most wives work as teachers, tutors, or baby-sitters.

Perhaps the most unique aspect of this *kolel* is the fact that first-year students receive no stipend. Though this places a strain on the younger students, they appear to accept and understand the reasoning behind this rule. It is the feeling of the administration that first-year students are likely to have smaller families, and it is, therefore, easier for their wives to support their study. Further, many have entered the *kolel* on a trial basis and will leave after the year has ended. Stipends should only be made available to those who "mature after marriage and decide that they want to continue to study earnestly before entering the job market."[127]

Those who remain beyond the first year are divisible in terms of their professional aspirations. Some will remain no more than about five years and will then seek a position either in education or in some commercial pursuit. For them, full-time study after marriage was an opportunity to mature within an atmosphere of academic contemplation.[128]

A second group will remain in the *kolel* for as long as ten years. These intend to become scholars and leaders of their community, filling positions in synagogues and institutions of higher Jewish learning. In 1982 there were twenty-five such young men in the Bobover Kolel, and their ranks are growing.

To facilitate entry into the fields of education and communal work, the *kolel* sponsors a "Yeshivas Hamasmidim" (diligent students). Three times each week, evening classes led by senior *kolel* fellows are held for younger students; their goal is to encourage a more intense commitment to study and ethical behavior. At the same time, these classes are a training ground for teaching and counseling younger students.

In addition, the *kolel* participates in a broad publication program under the auspices of the *yeshivah*'s office of publications. *Kolel* fellows are encouraged to pursue independent research during their evening sessions and to present the results of their research in *Kerem Shlomo*, a talmudic-halakhic journal published by the *yeshivah*. Biblical commentaries, responsa, studies in Jewish history and in contemporary Jewish life, and newly discovered rabbinic manuscripts are also published in the journal.[129]

Regarding programs of outreach, it must be recalled that the Bobover Kolel is located in the Boro Park section of Brooklyn, an area noted for its high concentration of Orthodox and *hasidic* Jews. Consequently, the introduction of programs to reach those outside the Bobover circle is difficult and may even be viewed with suspicion. In addition, the ready availability of a wide variety of services and programs in the Boro Park area obviates the need for additional undertakings of this kind.

Nevertheless, students of the Bobover Kolel do participate in several aspects of outreach that have had some impact upon their environment. They lead youth programs on Shabbat and holidays, under the title *Tiferes Bahurim*. Here, neighboring children are taught songs and stories relating to their studies or various elements of *hasidic* lore.

The *kolel* operates a free-loan society, which is directed and administered by *kolel* students. Study programs have been established for newly arrived Jewish immigrants, particularly those from behind the Iron Curtain whose contact with Jewish ritual and practice is minimal. Recently a group of loosely affiliated institutions under the auspices of Bobov was established in Israel, Belgium, and England, and several *kolel* fellows have been involved in this development.[130]

Within the *kolel* the atmosphere is quite serious. Approximately eighty students can be found there at any given time, and the *hasidic* mood is evident in their distinctive dress and the characteristic sing-song of their study aloud. There is a general feeling among the fellows that their institution has not received the visibility and acclaim it deserves. Thus, the opportunity for it to be portrayed in a work of this genre was met with much enthusiasm by students and faculty.

The students are friendly and hospitable and exhibit great pride both in their undertaking and in the contributions of the *kolel*. They seem to have a warm relationship with the *rosh hakolel*, who is a soft-spoken man hardly older than some of the senior fellows. However, he easily commands respect because he is the Bobover *Rebbe*'s son-in-law and is a recognized scholar with strong academic credentials of his own.

Alumni of the *kolel* take an important part in its activities, primarily because most retain membership in the Bobover community and live within walking distance of the institution. They attend regular classes offered to meet their schedules and participate in social programs on

Friday and Saturday evenings. They are actively involved in fund raising and contribute about 50 percent of the institution's budget. Their wives conduct luncheon programs and are equally supportive of the *kolel* and its activities.

In addition, special services are available for *kolel* alumni. Lectures have been delivered by leading faculty members and by such dignitaries as the *Rebbe*'s son, R.B.D. Halberstam. The *Rebbe* himself is available for counseling and consultation in both personal and professional matters. Programs are also available for children of alumni, and most send their children to Bobover elementary and secondary schools.

Accountability

The personal evaluation of the *yungeleit* (young men, or *kolel* fellows) by the *rosh hakolel* is a major method of determining their progress. Punctuality and regular attendance are criteria for measuring continued eligibility. Since the stipend is affected by absence or lateness, it is difficult to gauge sincerity by those means. But the *rosh hakolel* has introduced a method to motivate and induce student progress. At the completion of a particular unit, voluntary written examinations are taken, for which monetary prizes are awarded. The *rosh hakolel* takes pride in the results of these tests and has planned to extend them to the entire student body. By 1983 only thirty of the fellows submitted to the testing procedure, and there does not seem to be any additional objective method of accountability. As in similar institutions, the teachers rely on an intuitive evaluation of their students.[131]

8. KOLEL MESIVTA ZANZ

Like the *hasidim* of the Bobover community, those of Zanz trace their lineage to R. Hayyim Halberstam, rabbi of Nowy Sacz (Zanz) during the early nineteenth century. A grandson, R. Jacob Samson of Czchow, settled in the Transylvanian town of Klausenberg in 1917 and was later succeeded by R. Jekuthiel Judah Halberstam prior to World War II.[132]

The latter became known both by the title Zanzer and Klausenberger Rabbi, a position that he holds to this day. His wife and eleven children were killed in the Nazi onslaught, and he alone managed to escape and to reestablish his *hasidic* community in the Williamsburg section of Brooklyn just after World War II.

R. Jekuthiel remained in Brooklyn until 1956, when he founded Kiryat Zanz, a *hasidic* section of Natanya, Israel, which was intended to be the new home for his community. The *Rebbe* remained there for about ten years and developed a complex of educational, social-service, and health-care institutions in several parts of the country. He was forced to leave Israel for reasons of health, however, during early 1967, and he resettled in Union City, New Jersey, which has since become his headquarters.

In 1968 the Mesivta Zanz was opened in Union City as an extension of the main *yeshivah* founded in Israel. Four years later the *Rebbe* established a *kolel* there with only five students. The program has since grown to thirty students and has developed a reputation for innovation and quality.

Kolel Structure

The Kolel Mesivta Zanz is housed in one of two buildings that comprise the *mesivtah* of Zanz in Union City. It provides an auditorium, dining facilities, administrative offices, classrooms, and a dormitory. The *kolel* building also includes a study hall, synagogue, and library of about 5,000 volumes of Talmud, Jewish legal codes, commentaries, and a substantial collection of *hasidic* literature. The stated goal of the *kolel*, as summarized by the *Rebbe*, is for students

> to study two-and-a-half pages of Talmud and the commentaries per day, which adds up to 75 pages per month, and in about three years they will be able, with God's help, to complete the Talmud.[133]

Applicants to the *kolel* must be married and under the age of 30. They are graduates of the Zanz Yeshiva's lower divisions in Israel or in America, and they must present references from their prior instructors. Each applicant is interviewed by the *rosh hakolel*, who must determine whether the student is able to abide by the strict and rigorous program that the institution maintains.

Students are admitted on a three-tiered basis for a program of study spanning ten years. Initially, a commitment is made for three-and-a-half years, during which the new student is expected to cover the entire Talmud, as suggested in the *Rebbe*'s statement quoted above. After demonstrating this proficiency, the student is elevated to the next level of the program, where a further commitment of two-and-a-half years is made. During this time the student will review the entire Talmud once more, though in greater depth and with the inclusion of all classical commentaries.

Following the successful completion of this unit of the program, students are expected to remain for an additional four years. During the last stage of their studies, they review the Talmud once more and include all four sections of the *Shulhan Arukh*, the full code of Jewish law with its commentaries. The institution also plans to develop curricula incorporating other classical Jewish works, e.g., the Jerusalem Talmud and the Midrash. The result is a graduate who possesses vast knowledge of the sources and applications of Jewish ritual and practice. These will be the rabbis, teachers, and arbitrators of the Klausenberg community. The *Rebbe* stated: "Our men must replace the Jewish leaders murdered by the Nazis."[134]

Upon acceptance to the *kolel*, the student is eligible for a variety of stipends and fellowships, according to his initiative and academic ability. All students receive a base stipend of between $250 and $350 per month, depending upon the size of their family. In addition, a student may supplement this figure by attending a special morning session held from 5:00 A.M. to 7:00 A.M. daily, for which $150 is added to his monthly grant.

Those registered in the advanced programs of Talmudic study are allocated an additional $500 per month. In addition, fellows may receive up to $200 per month for remedial and tutorial work with younger students of the *yeshivah*. Thus, it is possible for fellows of the Zanz Kolel to increase their stipends to between $1,000 and $1,500 per month. Twenty of the program's thirty students now stand in that stipend range.[135]

The *kolel* does not provide housing for its students. However, students at the Zanz Kolel do not find this a problem. Housing is relatively inexpensive in Union City, and it is generally easy for fellows to secure comfortable accommodations near the *kolel* and within the *hasidic* community.

There is no active program of outreach, and it is difficult to ascertain what, if any, influence the *kolel* has had upon its immediate surroundings. Other than the Klausenberg community, Union City has only a marginal Jewish presence that comes in little contact with the *kolel* or its student body. Nevertheless, a few "outsiders" have been attracted to the *yeshivah* and participate in its program regularly.[136]

Program of Study

The Kolel Mesivta Zanz holds sessions twelve months per year, six days each week, with time off only for Jewish holidays. Punctuality and attendance are monitored carefully, although there is no formal system of penalties for regular tardiness or unexcused absence. Fellows study in *hevrutot*, but there is no *haburah* wherein students are required to lead sessions among their peers, though the idea is looked upon favorably by the administration, which is considering introducing such sessions.[137]

The day is divided into several study units. A morning *seder* begins at 5:00 A.M. and concludes just prior to morning prayers at 7:00 A.M. The regular program begins at 9:00 A.M. and continues until 1:00 P.M., followed by lunch and afternoon prayers. During this unit, fellows study the same Talmudic selections as the entire *yeshivah*, and are thus prepared to tutor younger students.

The afternoon *seder* ensues from 2:30 P.M. until 7:00 P.M. Here fellows study in their *hevrutot*, concentrating on convering volumes of Talmud in adherence with the primary goals of the institution. Evening sessions are voluntary, though it is not unusual for students to remain in the study hall until midnight in order not to fall behind.

The *Rebbe* delivers a lecture for students who have completed at least 600 folio of Talmud. Some twenty of the *kolel*'s students attend this session each week. In addition, lectures on *hasidism* are delivered each Thursday evening and at the afternoon meal each *Shabbat*. The entire student body attends these regularly.

The *kolel* does not grant any formal degrees, nor are its graduates ordained for the rabbinate. Students who seek such a title must prepare the appropriate texts on their own and at their own pace. They may then seek ordination from a rabbi within the Zanz community. By June 1982, five students of the Zanz Kolel had undertaken such a program and were ordained with the dual degree of *Yoreh Yoreh* and *Yadin Yadin*.

Faculty

The faculty of the kolel includes the *Rebbe*, his son, and his son-in-law, who serve as the *roshei hakolel*. Residence is provided for the faculty members, who receive a monthly salary of $1,000 plus health and insurance benefits.

Students

Students of the Zanz Kolel are almost uniformly graduates of the lower divisions of the Zanz Yeshiva. Most enter the *kolel* by the time they are 20 and have just recently married. Indeed, *kolel* study is seen as providing psychological support for the fellow's new marital status:

> The *Kolel* fellow has never read a newspaper, seen T.V. or listened to the secular radio. When he marries, this traumatic experience of meeting and living with a woman requires preparation. The *Rebbe* feels that every *hasidic* young man needs time to adjust and learning in the *Kolel* is helpful. Indeed, the wives admire their husbands who achieve the status of being in the *Kolel*.[138]

Kolel students range in age from 19 to 33 years. The younger fellows are newly married, and the senior fellows may have as many as seven children. All families are *hasidic* and adhere to the laws and customs of the Klausenberg community. Men and women dress modestly and are loyal to group norms.

The objective of the Zanz Kolel is to produce men with encyclopedic knowledge of Talmud and Jewish law. The administration encourages graduates to enter the fields of Jewish education and the rabbinate for the purpose of serving the Klausenberg community in particular and the Jewish people in general. Those who cannot complete the program enter the business world or become educators at the elementary and secondary levels. In exceptional cases, students have been extended special permission to enter the university and study medicine or law. In general, however, such training is discouraged in the strongest terms.[139]

The *kolel* has produced several volumes of Talmudic and rabbinic works, edited by the *Rebbe*.[140] Mention of the *kolel* and its activities appears prominently therein, and it is clear that its accomplishments are held in esteem by the community. One *kolel* graduate has produced a volume delineating the traditions of ritual slaughter and the laws of kosher meat preparation practised within the Zanz community.[141]

The atmosphere within the *kolel* is serious and controlled. The students are well aware of the stringent objectives that have been set for them. They are all aware that their presence in the *kolel* accords them considerable prestige within the community, and they feel morally obliged to make a serious effort to deserve such status. It is the feeling of the *rosh hakolel* that

> in every *Kolel* a few do not keep up with their learning as they should. The important thing is that even that minority is in the atmosphere of Torah and intensive learning and then something rubs off.[142]

Apparently, those who cannot cope with the strict pace generally leave the *kolel* within three years, i.e., before the initial set of examinations is given upon the first completion of the Talmud. There does not seem to be any implicit threat of expulsion, suspension, or financial penalty.

Special mention should be made of the importance imputed to *kolel* fellows as social and academic role models for younger students, and of the great contribution that *kolel* wives are said to make in supporting their husbands' aspirations and objectives. Both aspects have a profound impact upon the reputation of the institution and of its students. Thus *kolel* fellows

> set the goals for younger students to reach the point where they will be eligible
> to enter the *kolel*. . . . [Their] wives feel that they are partners in the great
> goal projected by the *Rebbe* . . . the history of Zanz should record the con-
> tributions of these women who build large families and are proud that their
> husbands are able to be part of the *kolel*.[143]

Unlike many other kolelim, the Kolel Mesivta Zanz has made a distinct
decision not to engage in programs of outreach toward those distant from
Jewish life. It is the *Rebbe*'s thinking that such activities distract students
from their learning and, considering the monumental tasks that have been
assigned to the *kolel*, such distraction cannot be tolerated.

He has illustrated his position through an engaging homily that bears
repeating:

> It is similar to the difference between two doctors. One is great and a special-
> ist in his field and has ability to heal the very sick who are on the verge of
> death. The second doctor is expert not at saving the desperately ill but at
> keeping the healthy person from illness. I am similar to that second doctor
> because the goal of our work is to teach those who are already involved in the
> study of Torah and faith the best traditional method so that they gain under-
> standing and to guard them against walking in deceptive paths. . . . Our
> *yeshivah* will not open its doors wide to everyone.[144]

The relationship between students and the *rosh hakolel* appears to be
warm and confidential, in that he is their direct link to the *Rebbe* and his
wishes. As one might expect of any *hasidic* community, trust and loyalty
toward the *Rebbe* are unquestioned, and study in the *kolel* is seen equally
as the fulfillment of the *Rebbe*'s wishes and as a means to broaden one's
intellectual and academic abilities.

There is no formal alumni organization or program for their participation in *kolel* activities. Several factors account for this absence. First, the
kolel is relatively new and its curriculum defines a course of study spanning some ten years. Second, most *kolel* alumni remain within the Klausenberg community and retain their loyalties to its leadership beyond any
identifications they might have with the *kolel*. Nonetheless, some 100 or
more students have spent time at the *kolel* and then left it for business or
other professional pursuits. They are not, strictly speaking, alumni, and it
is difficult to ascertain under what circumstances they left or what feelings
they harbor toward the institution.

Accountability

The Kolel of Zanz has taken several notable steps to assure accountability among its students, and this distinguishes it from most of its counterparts. Students must sit for written examinations each month. These are noncomprehensive and cover some seventy folio of Talmud. The test questions are composed by the *yeshivah* faculty, administered anonymously, and graded by other faculty assigned to the task. Thus, great care is taken to avoid favoritism—whether positive or negative.

Students are apprised of their standing regularly, and all grades, comments, and related materials are filed for future reference. This thrust toward objective accountability is taken very seriously by both students and administration. It is displayed proudly by the Zanz community as a model for similar institutions that seek to upgrade their standards.[145]

Nevertheless, it is not clear how accountability is implemented beyond the reporting of examination scores. There is no penalty for poor performance, nor is there any recognition for excellence. Such elements are left to such informal factors as personal status, peer pressure, familial influence, or the personality of the *rosh hakolel*. Thus, while an objective record of performance is being attempted and objectives are rather clearly defined, there does not seem to be any method of activating these variables in order to promote continued success or criticize poor performance. On balance, however, the Zanz Kolel has gone further than most others in this regard. In addition, informal pressures, unsystematic though they may be, should not be ignored as important sources of reward or penalty. Finally, one must consider the stated position of the *Rebbe* himself:

> We should learn from the secular world. If one must pass tests to remain in college, then definitely the *kolel*, whose objective is to learn Torah, must have a strict and responsible method.[146]

9. KOLEL AVREIKHIM OF THE HASIDIM OF GUR

The *hasidic* dynasty of Gur (pronounced Ger in Yiddish) was founded by R. Isaac Meir Rothenberg Alter (1789–1866). His father was a disciple of R. Levi Isaac of Berdichev and the rabbi of the town of Gur in Poland. R. Isaac Meir later became a disciple of R. Menahem Mendel of Kotsk. In 1859, R. Isaac Meir was accepted as the rabbi of the majority of the Kotsk *hasidim* after the death of R. Menahem Mendel. The dynasty existed in Poland from 1859 to 1939 and was transferred to Jerusalem, where it is one of the most powerful elements in the Agudath Israel movement. R. Isaac Meir was the author of one of the classic works of novellae on Talmudic tractates and the *Shulhan Arukh*. R. Isaac Meir himself is referred to by the name of his work, *Hiddushei ha-Rim* (Warsaw, 1875).

His grandson, R. Judah Aryeh Leib Alter (1847–1905), son of R. Abraham Mordecai (the eldest son of R. Isaac Meir), became the head of Gur in 1870. R. Judah Aryeh Leib is known by the name of his writings, *Sefat Emet* (1904–1908). He was succeeded by his son, Abraham Mordecai Alter (1866–1948), under whose leadership Gur *hasidism* achieved great heights in the decades preceding the Holocaust. He was one of the founders of Agudath Israel.

Abraham Mordecai visited Erez Yisrael many times and bought property there. He managed to escape from Gur to Warsaw in 1939 and was able to reach Erez Israel in 1940, where he died in 1948 during the siege of Jerusalem.

R. Abraham Mordecai's son, R. Israel Alter (1892–1980), who succeeded him, continued to build the influential Gur institutions in Israel and the United States. Among the institutions, the *yeshivot* stand in the forefront. The *kolel* in America is an innovation. It was founded in 1972 with a population of twenty fellows and now occupies a separate building in the Boro Park section of Brooklyn. The student body had grown to thirty by 1982.

R. Eliyahu Fisher, the *rosh hakolel*, responded to the question of why there were no *kolelim* in the Gur communities in Europe as follows:

> In Poland there was no *kolel* because every *soher* [businessman] was a great scholar. The method of learning among *Hasidim* in the *Klaus* [hasidic synagogue] was prevalent in Gur. There was no need for this kind of institution to provide married men with the opportunity to continue their Torah studies. It was also very difficult, if at all possible, to raise money for a *kolel*. The Jews were poor and barely existed in most small communities.[147]

R. Fisher enumerated four reasons for founding the Kolel Avreichim Gur.[148] First is the weakness of the present generation in Torah learning, a consequence of the Holocaust, which destroyed giants of Torah knowledge and the main centers of Torah study in Europe. Second, the *rosh kolel* expressed a strong desire to prepare men to serve the community as rabbis, teachers, *mohelim* (ritual circumcisers), and *shohetim* (ritual slaughterers). Third, role models who would influence generations to come must be developed. Fourth, and certainly not least, fellows are required to emigrate from the United States and to settle in Erez Yisrael by the time they complete their studies, in accordance with the mandate of the *Rebbe* of Gur.

The physical facilities available to the *kolel* include a *bet midrash*, which doubles as a *shtibl*. The library consists of about 500 volumes of Talmud, related literature, and *hasidic* works.

Kolel Structure

Admission procedures include an oral examination by the *rosh hakolel*. The candidate must show proficiency in the study of Talmud and the Codes. The eligible fellows must be married and preferably should be *hasidim* of the Gur community. Of the 30 men in the *kolel* in 1982, 20 were Gur *hasidim* and the rest were of various *hasidic* backgrounds such as Bobov and Viznitz. The fellows are accepted for an initial period of two years in the *kolel*. The age level of the *kolel* fellow ranges between 20 and 30 years of age.

Fellowships granted to the *kolel* men amount to a minimum of $200 per month for the newly married. Fellows with families receive $250 per week. Extra income is conferred upon those who pass written examinations on the material they study. The men receive $100 per exam. There are bonuses of $100 to $300 for holiday expenses, and a small work-study program exists. Arrangements are made with parents to subsidize the *kolel* men. [149]

The *kolel* fellows rent their own apartments in the Boro Park neighborhood of Brooklyn, New York. Rentals range from $250 to $500 per month and pose economic difficulty according to the *kolel* wives.

The Gur Kolel enjoys a close relationship with the surrounding community. *Kolel* fellows give lectures regularly to groups of laymen.

R. Eliyahu Fisher, *rosh hakolel*, responded to the query about outreach programs in the following manner:

> There are twenty men who regularly come to the *kolel* to hear *shi'urim* in the Jerusalem Talmud and the *Daf Yomi* [a page of Talmud is studied per day]. Our fellows are the lecturers in the summer camp conducted by the Gur community. Our *kolel yungeleit* are encouraged to reach out to other communities. Keep in mind that Gur is world-renowned as a friendly *hasidic* group. [150]

Program of Study

The learning day is divided into two formal sessions in the *kolel* building. The first *seder* starts at 9:30 A.M. and continues to 1:00 P.M. The second *seder* begins at 3:00 P.M. and ends at 6:00 P.M. In the evening the fellows study in pairs or individually in their homes. The fellows are required to attend six days per week. Their vacations include holidays and two months of Av and Elul (July and August).

The fellows study in *hevrutot*, which are organized by the students themselves. The language of study and instruction is Yiddish. When the fellows complete a unit of study, a lecture is delivered by the *rosh hakolel*. The *haburah* system is not practiced.

The curriculum emphasizes the mastery of *sugyot* in the Talmud. The starting point is the *Shulhan Arukh*. In previous years the focus was on *Orah Hayyim* and particularly the laws of *Shabbat*. From 1980 to 1982, the curriculum concentrated on the *Yoreh De'ah*, on the subject of *niddah*. In addition, the Gur fellows study *Shulhan Arukh Harav*. In the afternoon, a tractate of Talmud is studied (Kiddushin in 1982). The fellows also study works on *hasidut*, especially the writings of the *Sefat Emet*.

Some of the men approach the study of *Hoshen Misphat* in a manner similar to that of the Tauber Kolel of Monsey (see section 11). The Gur Kolel has introduced written tests for each unit, and $100 awards are bestowed upon those who pass with a grade above 90 percent.

The *kolel* has set goals that include the study of seven tractates (Shabbat, Pesahim, Eruvin, Gittin, Kiddushin, Kesubot, Nedarim) during the student's seven to ten years in the *kolel*.

The men are not required to receive *semikhah* (rabbinic ordination) at the end of the *kolel* program. However, they do apply to private rabbis in New York and Israel, and all the fellows have qualified for the degree of *Yoreh Yoreh*.

The *rosh hakolel* is involved in fund raising to cover the budget of the *kolel*. According to R. Fisher:

> In Poland there was no *kolel* because the average merchant was a scholar and so the concept of *kolel* is a new phenomenon among our *hasidim*. This makes it very difficult to raise money for the *kolel*. The *olam* [community] does not understand the importance of learning after marriage. They look at the *kolel* fellows as *batlanim* [time wasters] who should be out in the marketplace making a living instead of sitting and learning, supported by others. It is hoped that they will realize that this is the only way to develop scholars who will service our communities as rabbis, teachers, and judges.[151]

Faculty

The faculty is comprised solely of the *rosh hakolel*, who functions as *mashgi'ah*. The selection and appointment are made by the Gur *Rebbe* in Jerusalem. The salary of the *rosh hakolel* is about $1,500 per month and includes provisions for regular increases. The fringe benefits include Blue

Cross-Blue Shield protection. The *rosh hakolel* lives in a home that belongs to the Gur community, and it is provided for him rent free.

Students

All of the fellows are *hasidic* in their practices and come from Israel and the United States. The students have studied Torah from the age of 3 in *hasidic yeshivot* and have mastered six to eight tractates of Nezikin before entering the *kolel*.[152]

The method of learning is *hasidic*, i.e., concentration on mastering textual material leading to the practical application of religious law. The goal is to excel in the decisions of the codes of Jewish law and to know the sources of the laws. The dialectical method of study typified by the Lithuanian-type *yeshivot* is rare.

The families of the *kolel* fellows range from newly wed couples to families with five children. They are all obviously *hasidic*; the wives dress modestly in long-sleeved dresses, and the children are recognizable by their *peyot* (long sidelocks) and outer *zizit*. Gur *hasidic* men are distinguishable by their hats, knickers, and black socks. The male children also wear knickers and exposed socks. *Kolel* families live close to the Gur community institutions in Boro Park, and the *hasidic* families often are subsidized by the parents of the bride, who provide a dowry at her marriage.

The original (1972) career goal of the *kolel* fellows was to train teachers and *roshei yeshivah*. Since then, certain changes have occurred because of the *Rebbe*'s decision in Jerusalem. The philosophy of the *kolel* today includes the goal of settlement in Israel for the *kolel* family. Moreover, the *kolel* fellows are guided to enter the business world if they do not become professional educators and are urged to bring their studies into the marketplace. A few Gur *hasidim* have qualified for professional degrees in medicine and psychology.

The atmosphere of the *kolel* is friendly and seemingly without tensions. The fellows appear relaxed, and yet they study intensively. The rules are simple. Continuation in the *kolel* is based upon learning and punctuality. Attendance is checked by the *rosh hakolel* or by a fellow designated to act as *mashgi'ah* for this purpose, and deductions for absences are possible. Those who do not adhere to the rules may face expulsion. Since 1972, four fellows have been asked to leave. In view of the fact that joining the *kolel* endows the candidate with a measure of status, expulsion, threatened or actual, has considerable impact on the fellow and his family.

The relationship with the *rosh hakolel* is close since he is a contemporary of the older men in the *kolel* and a member of the *Rebbe*'s family. He serves as a role model for the younger men and has the reputation of a scholar and efficient administrator.

The *kolel* has published twenty pamphlets on *halakhic* subjects. The editor is R. Eliyahu Fisher. The material is culled from the answers to the test questions by the *kolel* fellows and covers the topics in the *Shulhan Arukh* studied by the men.

Since the *kolel* is only eleven years old, there is no substantial or organized alumni network at this date.

Accountability

The *kolel* fellows are mostly on their own. The supervising *rosh hakolel* claims to know each student personally and is able to gauge his progress. The written tests and the rule of punctuality serve as instruments to enforce accountability.

10. THE KOLEL PROGRAMS AT YESHIVA UNIVERSITY

Yeshiva University is the outgrowth of the first *yeshivot* founded in the United States. It traced its beginnings to the establishment of Yeshivat Etz Hayim, the earliest elementary institution in which both Jewish and secular studies were offered in 1886. It also incorporates the Rabbi Isaac Elchanan Theological Seminary (RIETS), America's first institution of higher Jewish studies, founded in 1897. The two were merged in 1915 primarily to forestall the bankruptcy of the latter, and the new organization was named the Rabbinical College of America.

Inadequate financial resources to justify the term "college" resulted in a reversion to the name Rabbi Isaac Elchanan Theological Seminary soon afterward, and the title has been retained to identify the primary programs of Jewish studies at Yeshiva University ever since.

The history and development of Yeshiva University in all its facets has been elaborately detailed elsewhere, and only a brief outline of the process is necessary here.[153] From the outset, it appears that the new institution was to be dedicated to a unification of both Jewish and secular scholarship under one roof. It was hoped that by producing rabbinic and lay leaders equally familiar with both worlds, Orthodoxy might survive the onslaught of American culture. This dedication was sealed by the choice of Dr. Bernard Revel as president of the institution in 1915 and has marked the development and structure of Yeshiva University ever since.[154]

Under Dr. Revel's administration, the institution grew and attracted numerous rabbinic scholars to serve on its regular faculty or to accept visiting appointments within its program. High school and college curricula were later added, and in 1937 a graduate school of Jewish studies was founded, based in part upon the scientific and historical study of Jewish culture and ritual. The inclusion of such units in tandem with traditional *yeshivah* learning was a radical undertaking, most unique in the cultural milieu being discussed here. The result was considerable tension with more conservative and traditional *yeshivah* leaders and rabbinical authorities elsewhere. This tension has also come to mark Yeshiva University in more contemporary times.

Dr. Revel's death in 1940 left the institution without leadership for almost three years. He was succeeded in 1943 by Dr. Samuel Belkin, a young member of the Talmud faculty. Dr. Belkin arrived in the United States at the age of eighteen, after having studied with the illustrious R. Israel Meir HaKohen of Radun, from whom he received his rabbinic ordination the previous year.[155] He proceeded to complete a doctorate in classics from Brown University and joined the faculty of RIETS in his mid-twenties. Under his leadership the institution was elevated to the status of a university, making it the first under Jewish auspices in the United States. A medical school, schools of social work, education, and psychology as well as a women's division all followed in their turn.

Dr. Belkin retired from the presidency in 1975 and died the following year. In July 1976 the presidency passed to Dr. Norman Lamm, an alumnus of the institution who had served for many years in the rabbinate and who also had a distinguished record as a writer and teacher of Jewish philosophy. Under Dr. Lamm's administration a law school was added to the university. In addition, a marked attempt to renew the school's commitment to traditional Jewish scholarship has been undertaken, and in this vein, *kolel* study at Yeshiva University has undergone a revival.

One more personality has left a profound mark on the quality of Jewish learning at Yeshiva University: R. Dr. Joseph B. Soloveitchik. Scion of an illustrious family of Lithuanian Jewish scholars, his father had been the *rosh yeshivah* at RIETS from 1928 until his death in 1941. R. Soloveitchik earned a doctoral degree from the University of Berlin, has served as Chief Rabbi of Boston since 1932, and succeeded his father as *rosh yeshivah* of RIETS.

Despite the official leadership of the university's president, it is R. Soloveitchik who is most closely analogous to the *roshei yeshivah* of other *kolelim* discussed in this work. Known simply as "the Rav," the Rabbi, by his students and disciples, it is he whom they seek for advice, and his scholarship and rabbinic acumen are held in far greater esteem than those of the president. The abilities of the university president are justifiably lauded by his supporters, and he is identified as the *rosh yeshivah*. Nevertheless, it is universally recognized that his position is principally one of administrative and academic leadership. The role of R. Soloveitchik is perceived as the more pristine, representing Yeshiva University's link to its more traditional counterparts and frequent detractors.

Tracing the development of the *kolel* within the Yeshiva University complex is no easy matter. Apparently, a *kolel* was begun in the early 1950s with only nine students. Little is said about the experiment, and it appears that the program lay dormant after a very few years. Most of these early students were not married, and each received a stipend of $50 per week. Some minor fund-raising efforts were undertaken on its behalf, and a *rosh hakolel* was appointed from among the ranks of the Talmud faculty.[156]

The program was renewed in 1961 under the direction of R. Aharon Lichtenstein, R. Soloveitchik's son-in-law. Under his tutelage the program enjoyed a period of success, and it was Dr. Belkin's intention to expand its activities and involve its fellows in guidance and remedial work with younger students.[157] However, R. Lichtenstein left to become *rosh yeshivah* at Yeshivat Har Ezion in the Judean Hills south of Jerusalem.

Finally, the *kolel* was continued in the late 1970s under the direction of R. Herschel Schachter, a young disciple of R. Soloveitchik and a graduate of RIETS. A major fund-raising effort has been undertaken, and several benefactors have come forward. A second program, geared specifically toward the study of Jewish civil and domestic law (*Hoshen Mishpat* and *Even Ha'ezer*), has recently been instituted under the leadership of yet another faculty member, R. Nisson Alpert. The program is known as the Yadin Yadin Kolel after the advanced degree that is conferred upon its graduates.[158] In addition, a third *kolel* has been established that places greater emphasis on independent research and service to the institution, under the direction of R. Aharon Kahn, another member of the Talmud faculty. This unit has also been matched with a benefactor.

Kolel Structure

All *kolel* programs at Yeshiva University are located at the university's main campus, a complex of buildings in the Washington Heights section of Manhattan in New York City. The *kolel* utilizes the *bet midrash* halls, several classrooms, dormitories, and a cafeteria, all of which are part of the general campus. In addition, fellows have access to university facilities, which include graduate programs in secular fields, placement services, career guidance, and recreational facilities. The university houses several libraries and special collections that are available to *kolel* students, a total of some 800,000 volumes.

In June 1983 there were forty-eight students in the various *kolel* programs sponsored by Yeshiva University. Applicants for admission into the Marcos and Adina Katz Kolel—which is the largest program—must hold an undergraduate degree in a secular field from an accredited university, a unique requirement in Orthodox programs of higher Jewish education.

In addition, the student must complete the RIETS *semikhah* program and sit for an oral examination with the *rosh hakolel*, R. Schachter. The latter is required to send his recommendations, in order of priority, to a formal acceptance committee. R. Schachter's decisions are generally accepted, and the number of students depends upon the availability of stipend funds.

Such requirements are similar for the Caroline and Joseph S. Gruss Kolel, also known as the Kolel Elyon (advanced *kolel*), although there has been some attempt to attract students from more traditional *yeshivah* programs outside of Yeshiva University. The program, begun in October 1982, has been unsuccessful in this attempt thus far. In pursuing this goal in the future, the requirement of college graduation may have to be mitigated or abolished altogether.

The Kolel L'Horaah (*Yadin Yadin*) is specifically geared towards the study of Jewish domestic and civil law. Applicants to this program are required to have completed their *semikhah* requirements and attained the rabbinic degree of *Yoreh Yoreh*. In addition, they must hold an undergraduate degree from some college or university program prior to entry in this *kolel*.[159]

There is no marriage requirement to enter any of the *kolel* programs. Upon acceptance into the Katz Kolel, single students are offered a stipend of ca. $1,900 per year plus free dormitory accommodations. Married fellows are given ca. $4,000 per year, but residential facilities are not available to them. Fellows of the Kolel Yadin Yadin program receive between $5,000 and $5,500 per year, and students in the new Gruss Kolel receive ca. $10,000 each year.

The main center of Yeshiva University is located in an area with a minimal Jewish presence. Indeed, though once a fashionable section of Manhattan, Washington Heights has suffered the urban blight common to many parts of New York and has consequently deteriorated. As a result, there is generally little opportunity for the *kolel* to have much impact upon the community.

Indeed, many of the *kolel* fellows do not live near the campus. They belong to various Jewish communities in other parts of New York City and are active within their congregations and social organizations. However, the institution does offer its fellows the opportunity to express creative energies through various outreach programs, discussed in greater detail below.

Program of Study

Fellows of all *kolel* programs at Yeshiva University study five days a week from 9:00 A.M. to 6:30 P.M. Those in the Katz Kolel are generally placed in a regular graduate-level *yeshivah* class. This means that they will prepare or review texts along with non-*kolel* students during morning hours and break for lunch about noon. The particular instructor assigned to class lectures from 1:00 P.M. to 3:00 P.M. on Mondays through Thursdays, and follows the tractates and texts chosen for the *yeshivah* at large.

From 3:00 P.M. to 6:30 P.M., *kolel* students meet in *haburot*. Students are required to lead these sessions on a rotating basis, roughly once every six weeks. The *kolel* follows the university's academic calendar, with time off for Jewish holidays and the summer months. A separate, voluntary program of summer study has also been instituted in conjunction with a summer camp that the university operates in Pennsylvania.

Kolel students follow the general *yeshivah* curriculum until 3:00 P.M. The texts for their afternoon sessions, however, are chosen by the *rosh hakolel* in consultation with the students in a process one fellow described as a "qualified democracy"—that is, the instructor always reserves the right to overrule his charges.[160]

In addition, the curriculum is partially set by the broad requirements of the rabbinic program in which all are simultaneously enrolled. Thus, to complete their rabbinic degree, students of the Katz Kolel are ordained at the completion of their studies and must, therefore, cover the requisite sections of *Shulhan Arukh* and sit for the same examinations as their non-*kolel* counterparts.

The *rosh hakolel* also uses this time to meet with the *haburot* and to present his own brief lectures. In addition, students are required to lead sessions as noted, and source material for these presentations are generally distributed in advance. Since most students of the Katz Kolel are single, they also participate in the regular rabbinic program for the bulk of their day.

The other two *kolel* programs are extremely small, numbering no more than five students each. During the morning and late afternoon sessions, these groups do not meet together but study in pairs at the two large *bet midrash* halls used by the entire *yeshivah*. The intention is for these fellows to serve as models for younger students while helping them with their studies and answering their questions.

For the bulk of the afternoon, however, these fellows meet in groups. Those studying for the *Yadin Yadin* advanced degree focus their effort on the particular sections of Jewish law codes relating to their fields of study. In 1982–83, those in the Kolel Elyon were studying Ketubot, though no formal program of study has emerged, nor has the curriculum been clearly determined.

Indeed, there appears to be some controversy regarding the objectives of the program generally, and it is clear that they have not yet been articulated by the administration. The words of R. Kahn, the *rosh hakolel*, are revealing:

> My feeling is that the emphasis should be on creative capacities. The men find this worrisome because of peer involvement. Some are atrophied in their creative thinking because they have had so much exposure to the Rav [R. Soloveitchik], who gives so much energy to *hidush* [novella], and they are accustomed to listening rather than projecting on their own. Others want a service component to this *kolel*. So meanwhile, since this is a three-year program, we have not undertaken any service projects which can start next year.[161]

The impression is that the program presently operates under considerable confusion, perhaps because it is new. However, it also appears that funding was successfully sought before a clear vision and set of objectives were articulated, and the organization is now undergoing the slow and difficult process of developing its identity.[162]

Faculty

As noted, there are three *roshei kolel*, each attached to another program, and no formal coordination exists among them. Each is also on the faculty of the regular *yeshivah* program and under the immediate supervision of the director of RIETS and the president of the university. In addition, regular faculty members are occasionally called upon to deliver lectures or supervise the work of *kolel* fellows.

For their services, each *rosh kolel* receives a salary of between $15,000 and $20,000 per year. Various fringe benefits such as health, medical, and life insurance as well as a retirement plan are provided. The *kolel* does not provide housing for its faculty.

Students

Of the 48 students in the various *kolel* programs at Yeshiva University in 1983, only 8 were married. The latter were all in their first year of marriage, and none had children. Many were the sons of rabbis and other communal functionaries who had themselves studied at Yeshiva University and who may have been the graduates of *kolel* programs there or elsewhere. In addition, the wives of these students were almost all graduates of Stern College, the undergraduate women's division of the university.

One of the more unique aspects of the *kolel* student population is the substantial proportion of fellows who are graduates of the James Striar School (JSS) of the university. This program is specifically geared toward students of little or no Orthodox Jewish background who have attended public elementary and secondary schools. Thus, many *kolel* students had almost no contact with intensive Jewish education five years earlier. This is particularly characteristic of the Katz Kolel.

There has been some ambivalence regarding the impact of these *baale teshuvah* and newcomers to Jewish life. For some, their presence in the *kolel* is a tribute to the institution and its various outreach programs. It also indicates the success of JSS in raising the academic standards of a largely ignorant student group in but a few years. For others, however, the presence of these students is a distraction that necessarily lowers the level of *kolel* study, as the group proceeds at the pace of the slowest student. Indeed, this appears to be the consensus of *kolel* fellows, whose views are reflected in the following sentiment:

> The effect of the YP and YC [regular *yeshivah* students] men in the *kolel* plus the JSS has lowered the level of the learning and it is my feeling that the *kolel* is not as strong as it was even three years ago when I entered. On the whole, the *hasmadah* [commitment] has not diminished. In fact, the men are highly motivated. But in terms of knowledge, students who were part of the *kolel* in former years had learned longer and knew more.[163]

Unlike students at many other institutions under discussion here, it is not uncommon for students at the Katz Kolel to have jobs or to be taking graduate degrees in various secular programs within Yeshiva University or elsewhere. Though officially inappropriate, the administration appears to condone these efforts and to adjust stipends according to the availability of outside income to the given student. Wives often work as well, and there appears to be some unhappiness about the considerable time commitment required of their husbands. Nevertheless, they also take pride in their husbands' commitment to Torah and Jewish study.[164]

There is no formal service component attached to study in the Gruss Kolel, though it has been suggested, as noted above. Fellows are not required to follow any particular career pattern, although many are interested in Jewish education or the rabbinate. To facilitate that choice, the general *yeshivah* division offers applied and apprentice courses relating to the rabbinate, communal service, and education. Practitioners in these fields lead workshops, and internships can be arranged for interested students. In addition, full graduate programs are available in Jewish education for the student who wishes to complete a professional degree in addition to his *kolel* study.

Outreach is a major aspect of Yeshiva University generally, and *kolel* students participate in many of its facets. The Torah Leadership Seminar and the Counterpoint Program are two projects undertaken by the university's Communal Service Division. The goal of these projects is to make regular contact with those distant from Jewish life in the United States, Australia, Central America, and other far-flung parts of the world. Indeed, many young people begin their careers at Yeshiva University through initial contact with one of these programs, which must, therefore, be seen as a recruitment effort as well. Some *kolel* students who are graduates of the James Striar School began their journey toward Jewish culture at one or another outreach session.

Kolel students serve as faculty, advisors, and counselors at these programs, delivering lectures, leading study or discussion groups, and meeting with young participants informally. They have had a profound influence upon many such students and have later been invited to perform similar services at weekend programs for local teenagers in their home towns. In addition, the experience has proven invaluable for those fellows who later enter Jewish education or who work with youth professionally.

In addition, fellows have been involved in a more academic project oriented toward adult education outside the New York City area. The Jewish communities of Boston and Washington, D.C., have organized annual programs of study in which scholars-in-residence are invited to deliver lectures and lead sessions. The master instructor has generally been a faculty member—in Boston, R. Soloveitchik himself—and *kolel* fellows offer classes in Talmud, Jewish law, and Bible to men and women of a variety of ages and academic backgrounds. The program has been most successful both for the exposure it offers the fellows as well as the practical experience in the field of education.

The atmosphere at the Yeshiva University *kolelim* appears uniformly warm and serious. Students view themselves as part of a special mission, which creates a strong sense of solidarity. Perhaps most important is their relationship with their respective *roshei hakolel* who, in the case of the Gruss and *Yadin Yadin* programs, are required to interact with a select number of students.

In this regard, the following student assessment of the *rosh hakolel* is typical: "In addition to being a friendly, helpful person, our *rosh hakolel* is a veritable walking encyclopedia of Torah knowledge. He has a phenomenal grasp of every topic and is highly systematized."[165]

In 1983, there were approximately 250 alumni of various *kolel* programs at Yeshiva University. They are organized along with other rabbinic graduates of the institution in the Rabbinic Alumni of Yeshiva University, and there is no separate *kolel* alumni association. Members of the Rabbinic Alumni meet regularly and have direct contact with a university staff member who helps organize their activity. No programs oriented specifically toward *kolel* alumni and their needs have been undertaken, and it does not appear that any are planned.

Accountability

There appears to be a high degree of accountability in all *kolel* programs at Yeshiva University, especially as compared to most other *kolelim* cited in this study. However, as with other aspects of this institution, methods vary with the particular *kolel* program.

As noted, the students of the Katz Kolel are also enrolled in the regular rabbinic program leading to ordination at the end of three years. They must pass a series of five major written examinations dealing with the variety of codes relating to Jewish ritual and dietary laws.

In addition, students take a series of four examinations each year, composed by the *rosh hakolel* and directly related to the texts and curriculum of their *kolel* study. Finally, each fellow is required to deliver a lecture to his *haburah* roughly once every six weeks, under the supervision and direction of the *rosh hakolel*. There can be little doubt that this constitutes adequate accountability at this level of study.

A similar situation is evident at the Yadin Yadin Kolel. The four students in this small group in 1983 had all completed their regular rabbinic studies and were genuinely hand-picked. The curriculum in this program is clear, and students complete it by undergoing a lengthy oral examination in the various sections of *Shulhan Arukh* that relate to civil and domestic rulings. Though not as systematic, such a program of accountability is likely to suffice as long as the student population remains small.

Accountability in the Gruss program appears to suffer from the same malaise that besets its curriculum of study and its objectives generally. Here again, the program is small, and the *rosh hakolel* is able to monitor each fellow's attendance and performance. Yet there seems to be no standard by which to measure performance. Students do lead *haburot*, but a clearer and more systematic approach to evaluation would help sharpen the mission of this program. Nevertheless, in the words of its *rosh hakolel*:

> We are aware of their [the fellows'] mental capacities, memory skills, and accumulated knowledge. They need no tests for accountability, but we rather prefer *haburot* as the method of study. These men would have no problem with tests because all have gone through the system of testing. The novel experience for them is to create and write.[166]

11. KOLEL MECHON HAHOYROA

Kolel Mechon Hahoyroa is located in Monsey, New York, and is popularly called the Tauber Kolel after its founder and primary supporter, R. Azriel Tauber. In many ways it is the most unusual of all the institutions of this study. Its approach to higher Jewish education, its independence from a larger institution or community, and the circumstances that surround its creation all set it apart not only from *kolelim* elsewhere, but from much of prior Jewish education both in the United States and abroad.

Unlike most other *kolelim*, the Mechon Hahoyroa does not trace its beginnings to a major European *yeshivah* of the last century or to a large *hasidic* community. Indeed, it was founded as a break from these institutions by one who was dissatisfied with the quality of their graduates. Its primary philosophy is that *kolel* fellows can be motivated to high levels of expertise and accomplishment, but need substantial material incentives and a strict program of accountability to produce optimally.

Azriel Tauber is the graduate of several *hasidic yeshivot* and is an ordained rabbi. His primary field of endeavor, however, is real estate investment and development. Commercial expertise has leavened his approach to the world of higher Jewish education with pragmatism. It has long been surmised that the philanthropy invested in *kolelim* and their students has not yielded adequate returns in terms of scholarship and service, according to Tauber. He attributes this failure to several factors. In the first instance, the structure of *kolel* study generally tends to discourage critical evaluation of its methods and results. Students and supporters simply develop school loyalties and the assumption emerges that the mere existence of a *kolel* is a sign that serious scholarship is taking place there.

He is also dismayed by what he considers unprofessional and haphazard treatment that *kolel* students suffer. How can one expect serious study when fellows are paid a pittance and are required to fend for themselves through their wives' employment and parental largess? And it is still more demeaning when even this pittance is not delivered on time or is distributed as charity.

His most severe criticism is reserved for the general lack of systematic accountability and formal evaluation common to most *kolelim* and the *yeshivot* they represent. His words are telling:

> What is the *heter* [license] for putting a few *yungeleit* into a room and *schnor* [beg] money for that *kolel* without demanding accountability, without exams and without proper supervision? Of course there should be a sense of responsibility toward the *yungeleit*; i.e., they should receive what you promised them. They should also be responsible to produce the utmost that they can deliver scholastically and not just sit or wander for years. There is even a greater responsibility to the people from whom money is being collected, so their well-meaning charity should be used properly.[167]

It was on this basis that Tauber decided to create the Kolel Mechon Hahoyroa in 1976. In so doing, he saw himself as fulfilling several rabbinic dicta. He identifies himself as the modern-day Zebulun, who is said to have entered into a partnership with his brother, Issakhar, whereby the former would financially support the Torah study of the latter. In such an arrangement, both partners shared the theological fruits of labor and eternal reward.[168]

Azriel Tauber is further convinced that the intention of such higher Jewish learning is not to attract large numbers of students, but to cater to the individual who will later emerge as a great interpreter of Jewish law. Once more citing a rabbinic source, he recalls the dictum that a thousand may enter the hall of learning, but only one exceptional scholar will emerge. The goal of the study hall, he concludes, is to produce that one exceptional student who will be "the decider of Jewish law."[169]

Kolel Structure

The Kolel Mechon Hahoyroa is located in the lower level of a private home in Monsey, New York, an area that has developed a large and active Orthodox Jewish community over the past twenty years. One room serves both as *bet midrash* and library, housing a collection of some 1,000 volumes in the traditional areas of Jewish law, Talmud, and commentaries. The *kolel* began with 4 students in 1976 and by mid-1982 had grown to 15.

The original fellows were chosen by R. Eliezer Tauber, Azriel's brother, who serves as *rosh hakolel*. Particularized entrance requirements have not been articulated, though they are very much in keeping with the original intent. Applicants must already be ordained with the degree *Yoreh Yoreh*. Since this area was frequently emphasized in similar programs, the Taubers saw a need to develop scholars with expertise in more neglected topics of study, such as business and civil codes as well as marital and domestic law.

Applicants must be married and show letters of reference from their prior instructors or from directors of other *kolelim* in the case of transfer applications. They must also sit for an interview and examination prior to acceptance. Perhaps most important is the applicant's willingness to commit himself contractually to the completion of all four sections of the *Shulhan Arukh*, even should such an undertaking require ten years of study, as it often does.

Upon acceptance, students receive $700 per month plus an additional $50 per month per child, with increments based on a series of examinations discussed below. In June 1982, the typical fellow received approximately $1,000 per month, and $1,500 was not without precedent. It is clear that the students of the Kolel Mechon Hahoyroa receive stipends that are substantially higher than those extended by other *kolelim*. In addition, the opportunity for financial advancement based on proven excellence is considerable.

Aside from their stipends, fellows are enrolled in a Blue Cross-Blue Shield health plan, half of which is subsidized by the *kolel*. They are also encouraged to apply for Medicaid. Bonuses are available for students who prepare responsa and who serve as consultants for community inquiries. The *kolel* provides no housing, and students must find local apartments or commute from New York City.

Though small and relatively unknown within its own environs, the *kolel* has already had a profound impact upon the quality and structure of higher Jewish study elsewhere. As a result of several magazine and newspaper reviews of its program and the successful examination of its students by leading rabbis in Israel, the Kolel Mechon Hahoyroa has generated considerable interest.[170]

Firstly, support has come from many people who agree that accountability is a most important aspect. Secondly, we have been asked to introduce our program to other *kolels*. We have established the same kind of *kolel* for Sephardic students in Jerusalem, in Ashdod, and to date we have seven *kolels* which have accepted our system of testing.[171]

In addition, Azriel Tauber has offered financial aid to those institutions that have incorporated some of their views, e.g., the Klausenberg Kolel. In some instances, almost 50 percent of the student's stipend is subsidized by the Taubers, resulting in a substantial increase. These subventions are offered, however, on the consideration that strict accountability is maintained, and funds are distributed in a timely and professional manner. As an indirect result, some other *kolelim* in New York and in Israel are alleged to have raised their stipends because the Tauber system has become an important standard.

The *kolel* has also established a *bet din*, or court of arbitration, to adjudicate conflicts on the basis of Jewish law. The *kolel's bet din* is composed of *kolel* students and has won some acceptance within the local community. Papers have been prepared regarding the status of wills, investment documents, securities, and bonds in the context of Jewish law. In addition, monetary disputes have been submitted for adjudication by those who prefer to settle their claims outside the secular judicial system and in accordance with Jewish precedent.[172]

Program of Study

The typical day at the Kolel Mechon Hahoyroa begins at 5:30 A.M. and is divided into three *sedarim*. The first *seder* extends to 8:00 A.M. There is then a two-hour recess for prayers and the morning meal. Studies resume at 10:00 A.M. and continue until 2:30 P.M., when there is a 45-minute adjournment for lunch. The final *seder* begins at 3:15 P.M. and ends at 7:30 P.M. The program gives this *kolel* one of the longest study days of all, with all work done at the institution itself.

The fellows generally study in *hevrutot*, though some prefer to work independently. The *rosh hakolel* serves primarily as supervisor and consultant. He offers no lectures, nor does he lead sessions of discussion and analysis. The *rosh hakolel* also records attendance. Unexcused absences result in the deduction of $12 per month from the fellow's stipend. Attendance is required twelve months per year, with time off only for holidays.

Unlike most other subjects of this study, emphasis at this *kolel* is placed upon the study of *Hoshen Mishpat* and *Even Ha'ezer*, sections of the Jewish codes that deal with monetary, civil, and domestic practice. Students are expected to cover, with standard commentaries, twenty chapters per month and to master the underlying sources, ramifications, and applications of the law up to contemporary times. A special consultant is employed to prepare Hebrew examinations in these subjects, as well as in other texts.

The *kolel* confers the degree of *Yadin Yadin*. There is a marked preference, however, for the fellow to seek ordination before a rabbinic court, as was recently (1982) undertaken successfully in Jerusalem and Bnai Brak. In such cases, the *kolel* will provide the examining body with records of the student's examination scores and attendance.[173]

Faculty

The single faculty member is the *rosh hakolel*, who performs duties akin to a *mashgi'ah* elsewhere, and does not appear to serve any traditionally academic functions. His salary is $200 higher than the best stipend, and he is included in the aforementioned health plans, whose costs are borne by the *kolel*.

Students

By June 1982, there were fifteen students at the Kolel Mechon Hahoyroa, the majority of *hasidic* backgrounds, particularly stemming from the Gur, Zanz, and Satmar communities. Before coming to the *kolel*, all were involved in Torah studies elsewhere, and one was a Talmud instructor in Jerusalem.

These students, ranging in age from 25 to 40, will spend at least ten years of study at the *kolel*. All are married and have been ordained at some other institution. All have beards and *peyot* and dress in black.

Kolel families typically have four to five children who attend one of the more traditionally Orthodox primary or secondary *yeshivot* in Monsey, a suburban community in which a rich variety of such institutions is available. Given the generally higher scale of stipends offered to these *kolel* students, it is less often necessary for their wives to work outside the home, and the latter are consequently somewhat more content with their roles as mothers and homemakers. The women stem from similar backgrounds and dress in the very modest fashion characteristic of such communities.[174]

Given the length and intensity of the program, little concern or consideration has been given to career goals. Obviously, the nature of the program and curriculum tends to prepare and orient students of this *kolel* towards careers as scholars and interpreters of Jewish law, beyond the educational or communal interests expressed by students elsewhere. Nevertheless, students are not obliged to commit themselves formally to such goals, and for its part, the *kolel* requirements include attendance, study, and successful examination.

The *kolel* does not sponsor a program of outreach per se. The explanation is quite simple: "Our concentration is completely inwards. Our goal is to develop great scholars and during this phase of their lives no distractions, no matter how important they may be, are permitted."[175]

Yet the institution has established an extension division not unlike outreach programs elsewhere, except for the fact that fellows themselves are not directly involved. It appears that the *kolel* has received various applications from younger students in secondary or undergraduate institutions. Though these students are not yet eligible for *kolel* study, the Taubers have extended consideration to them by creating a *mekhinah* (preparatory) program to develop these youngsters in the skills and disciplines necessary for a career at the *kolel*.

One aspect of the *mekhinah* program is the Shas Kolel, in which students are required to gain expertise in Talmudic study and undergo examinations on twenty folio pages per month. These students receive $500 per month with increments for scores of 90 percent and above. Students who can maintain this pace for two years will be admitted to the regular *kolel*.

Younger students may participate even while still enrolled at other institutions. Thus, a teenager recommended by his own *yeshivah* may sit for an examination in fifty folio of Talmud with basic commentaries. The examinations are comprehensive in that each test presumes competence in the one that preceded it.

For the successful completion of each test, the student is credited with $90. The program extends for ten examinations, at which time he has completed 500 folio of Talmud and accrued credits of $4,500. This amount is placed in an interest-bearing escrow account which the student may receive at the time of his wedding.

Ten such students have completed two sets of examinations, indicating mastery of more than 1,000 folio. A bonus has been added for a total credit of $10,800. Students who aspire to *kolel* fellowship may leave the money in their accounts and later receive it as part of their monthly stipend. Such pilot programs have been introduced at *yeshivot* in Brooklyn and northern New Jersey.[176]

A system of this type has also been introduced in Jerusalem as part of the Veshinantem Program. As of 1983, some 200 students are participating and approximately 20 are tested each week. The examinations are prepared by a *kolel* consultant and are presently being computerized. Already $22,500 has been invested, 50 percent of which has been extended in the form of credits to participants. Though this may not be a formal and traditional outreach program, it certainly qualifies as an attempt to extend the values and benefits of Torah study beyond the walls of the *kolel* itself.[177]

Despite the intense emphasis upon examinations and close supervision, the day-to-day atmosphere of the *kolel* seems free of the tensions and anxieties that might be expected. The fellows are quite serious about their work, yet they do not appear competitive, and their relationships seem quite congenial to the observer. Undoubtedly, any anxieties that may have arisen have been mitigated by the considerable length of time the fellows have worked together in this small group.

This same congeniality is also extended to the *rosh hakolel*. He is a contemporary of the students and is treated with respect for his scholarship and for the fact that he serves as liaison with the primary benefactor of the *kolel*, his brother. Unlike the relationship between fellows and the *rosh hakolel* elsewhere, he is seldom sought for personal guidance or direction.

This may result from several factors. The *rosh hakolel* of Mechon Hahoyroa is neither a lecturer nor an instructor. Study and research at the institution are largely undertaken independently and outside his direct leadership. In many respects, his own responsibilities are more administrative and supervisory than they are academic. In addition, many of the students at the *kolel* are of *hasidic* stock and belong to one or another *hasidic* community. Their activities at the *kolel*, though a vital part of their lives, are primarily academic and undertaken within the context of their community. Consequently, when they are in need of advice or direction, they are far more likely to consult with their own rabbinic authorities or communal leaders.

The institution is still relatively new and its program is arduous and long. As a result, to date (1985) there are no alumni nor are there any immediate plans for programs or organizations through which graduates might retain their ties with the *kolel*. The *kolel* has published a lengthy volume of student work in areas of Talmud and *halakhah* entitled *Yisaschar B'ohalekhah*. There will doubtless be more such volumes in the future.[178]

Accountability

As described above, the most distinctive element of the *kolel* Mechon Hahoyroa is its system of accountability and monetary incentives. Unlike other subjects of this study, the *kolel* administers monthly examinations based on given sections of study and as part of a formal contract with the students. In addition, students are penalized for absences and rewarded for their success on examinations. The institution has set unusually high standards in its assignments to students and has found that with the necessary incentives and a selective student body, fellows of the *kolel* can produce considerably more than their counterparts elsewhere.

The sole weakness in the system is that the consequences of failure are not clearly articulated. One suspects that a student who is consistently found to be lacking would be asked to resign from the program. No structure has been established for such an eventuality, and as yet no such case has occurred.

One might also be wary of the potential corruptibility as such a system grows and becomes more complex. On the one hand, should the *kolel* encourage study for the sake of monetary reward? On the other hand, might such strict accountability encourage dishonesty in preparing and sitting for examinations? At present, however, the *kolel* appears quite successful and represents a singular and innovative experiment.

12. KOLLEL HORABONIM

Kollel Horabonim is located in Monsey, New York, a suburban area some thirty miles north of New York City with a large and varied Jewish population. It was founded by R. Leib Landesman in 1973. A graduate of Yeshiva Torah Vodaath, where he was ordained rabbi, R. Landesman originally intended to build an institution similar to other *kolelim* cited in this study, i.e., a place where young married men could devote themselves full-time to their Torah studies. This goal was soon replaced, and the result has so veered from the norm that the title may genuinely be a misnomer here.

Primarily, students of the Kollel Horabonim are engaged in detailed research regarding practical questions of Jewish personal status, and marital and domestic law. Most of these questions have been forwarded to its dean by way of referral. Each of its students has already been ordained and the *kolel* offers no formal degree program, nor does it encourage its fellows to seek ordination privately.

What is most unique about this institution—and what raises the issue of its legitimacy as a *kolel*—is the fact that its students only meet two hours each day and are often enrolled simultaneously in other *yeshivot* or *kolelim*. In this respect, Kollel Horabonim is more a research center, which has chosen the title *kolel* to increase its acceptability within the community.

Kolel Structure

The Kollel Horabonim, or rabbis' *kolel*, is so named because all of its fellows are already ordained rabbis. It is housed in the lower level of R. Landesman's private home. The *kolel* room includes a collection of some 1,000 volumes of Talmudic and responsa literature. Of course, students are also encouraged to use their own or local libraries for their research.[179]

Applicants to the program must be married and have been ordained at a recognized *yeshivah* or by a leading rabbinic authority. Preference is given to applicants who have studied at other *kolelim* within the past few years. It is acceptable for the fellows to continue their studies elsewhere as part of a day program, since the *kolel* requires evening attendance only.

Applicants must sit for an extensive interview with R. Landesman and bring references from former instructors. The *rosh hakolel* often confers with outside referees regarding individual applicants or observes them at their present place of study. The final decision, however, is solely his.

The institution began with four students in 1973, and in 1982 there were twelve fellows at the *kolel*, ranging from 25 to 40 years of age. The student population is held at this level, and new students are admitted only upon the withdrawal of a present registrant. This has occurred only five times since the *kolel*'s inception. Consequently, turnover and outside recruitment are minimal.[180]

Upon acceptance, fellows receive $125 per month. If research is required beyond the regular daily hours, students receive ca. $10 per hour for their time. The *kolel* provides no housing for its students. All fellows find accommodations in the nearby area, which has a substantial population of *kolel* fellows from several neighboring institutions.

Though there is no formal outreach program and *kolel* students do not direct adult education activities as part of their responsibilities, the presence of the institution has had an impact on some segments of the neighboring community. The object of the *kolel* is to provide an authoritative center to which problems of family life and personal status may be referred. In this respect, the community has availed itself of the services the *kolel* may offer.

Endorsed by leading rabbinic figures of both the *hasidic* and *yeshivah* elements of Jewish life, the *kolel* claims to add a new dimension to local community affairs while attempting to service a worldwide need. Though a Jewish community has thrived in Monsey for many decades, the *kolel* was responsible for the execution of the first *get* (Jewish bill of divorce) there in 1975. This was accomplished by overcoming problems of wording, location, and detail that had heretofore appeared insurmountable.[181]

A sampling of questions that have been forwarded to the *kolel* for research has been appended to this unit.

Program of Study

Fellows attend sessions of research and study at the Kollel Horabonim five days each week, twelve months a year, with time off only for Jewish holidays. Daily programs are held in the evening from 8:00 P.M. to 10:00 P.M., and punctuality is monitored carefully, No lectures are delivered. Fellows study in *hevrutot* chosen voluntarily.

The curriculum is not defined, nor is it in any way standardized as in most other *kolelim*, except to note that all topics covered relate to domestic and marital law. Rather, the program of study is set according to inquiries that have been forwarded through rabbis or lay persons. Research is then divided and assignments are made by the *rosh hakolel*.

Upon receiving an inquiry or referral, students begin their research by reviewing the Talmudic sources for prior decisions on the topic. Concentration then turns to the various collections and codes of Jewish law, contemporary works, and more recent precedents. The emphasis on issues of practical need is most attractive to the fellows, excites their interest, and results in greater depth and detail in their research.[182]

Upon completion of their research, R. Landesman gathers the decisions and comments of the students and then composes a response to the inquiry. Research is normally done during the program's regular hours. In the event of emergency, R. Landesman will authorize extra research, for which fellows are remunerated separately, as noted above.

Aside from inquiries and referrals, the *kolel* maintains a regular program of study aimed at supporting research and expertise in the areas of concentration.

> In the regular *seder* of learning, when we are not researching a problem, we start with the *Shulhan Arukh*, go back to the Talmudic sources, proceed to the *Tur* [predecessor of the *Shulhan Arukh*, on which many of its decisions are based], and then back to the Code with its commentaries. We seldom go to responsa literature unless we are called up to answer a question.[183]

In addition, students are expected to review Talmudic tractates relevant to domestic and marital law. Particular emphasis is placed upon the study of the tractate Kiddushin. According to the *rosh hakolel*, this section can generally be reviewed in the course of six to nine months, if there are not many inquiries or other distractions that must take precedence.

As noted, the *kolel* confers no degrees and all applicants must have already been ordained elsewhere. In 1982, 8 of its 12 students were ordained by R. Moshe Feinstein, a leading rabbinic authority and head of Yeshiva Tifereth Yerushalayim.

Faculty

There is but one faculty member who is also dean, administrator, and fund-raising director. Until 1980, the last activity filled much of his time. However, several benefactors have emerged since then, and financing the institution has been somewhat easier as a result. Information regarding the salary, benefits, and provisions for the *rosh hakolel* was not available.[184]

Students

The students of Kollel Horabonim are graduates of *yeshivot* in the United States or Israel. They have all studied at other *kolelim* and, as noted, many are simultaneously enrolled elsewhere. Half are of *hasidic* background and three are college graduates, a fact that is not circulated given the generally negative perceptions of secular education common among those whom the *kolel* must service.

The families of these students typically include three to four children and a wife who teaches at a local *yeshivah*, generally at the primary level. Since these fellows are older than most *kolel* students and have other sources of income, parents do not support them. The wife's salary is their primary source of income, aside from the *kolel* stipends. Children attend local *yeshivot* as well, and the families do not generally socialize, given the pressures of time.

Though their schedule places many burdens upon the family and there is a clear need to sacrifice materially, students believe that the *kolel* experience has been beneficial to their marriages and family lives, as is evident in the following comment:

> Children are influenced by the awareness of the father who also leaves to go to study Torah every morning and evening. There is a sense of pride which is what the *kolel* parents want their children to have about Torah learning. Moreover, they see that learning Torah is not reserved for children but is an adult activity.[185]

The *kolel* does not actively encourage its students to pursue particular career goals, nor does it involve itself in any placement activities. Nevertheless, there exists an unspoken understanding that graduates of the *kolel* will enter higher Jewish education or serve in the capacity of *dayan* (rabbinic judge). Clearly, such positions do not abound and competition is expected to be keen. This concern is counterbalanced by their faith in the vitality of the Jewish community and the projected increase in the numbers of those who will need Jewish education in the future.

The atmosphere of study at Kollel Horabonim is serious and surprisingly enthusiastic, considering the late hours. There is an atmosphere of respect and an esprit de corps among the students that extends to the *rosh hakolel*, who is roughly their age. Nevertheless, most students view their participation in the program as a welcome addition to their income. Alumni do not maintain links as a result.[186]

Questions have been raised regarding the title assumed by this establishment: Does it genuinely deserve the name *kolel*?

On the one hand, observers have lauded the institution as one that confronts potentially explosive issues and provides a genuine service to the Jewish community both locally and elsewhere. They note the willingness of rabbinic authorities to refer complex inquiries to Kollel Horabonim, and they praise the accomplishments of the institution in both applied and academic concerns.[187]

Its service notwithstanding, however, it is difficult to justify the use of the term *kolel* for an institution that requires only two hours of daily study by its fellows and which utilizes their talents for the research of specific *halakhic* problems. Its program is set almost entirely by the referrals it receives, and there are neither lectures nor presentations. In the words of one local critic who preferred anonymity: "This *kolel* is nothing more than a private group operated by one man who has legitimized his activities by organizing a '*kolel*.' "[188] While his tone is overly harsh, the underlying criticism appears well-founded.

Accountability

Since R. Landesman functions as the sole support of this *kolel* and the *kolel* serves a pragmatic cause—the solution of an actual problem of the moment—each fellow must contribute to the research. The small size of the group makes it simple for the *rosh hakolel* to judge the work of each fellow and his value to the project. Hence, although there are no objective criteria such as tests, accountability is nevertheless exercised in the relationship between the dean and the fellows.

INQUIRIES REFERRED TO KOLLEL HORABONIM*

1. May a Cohen marry a *balas tshuva*?

---

*Some of the questions have been changed to retain the anonymity of those involved. The essence, however, remains the same. The spelling is that of the official school version.

2. A wife cannot have children. Is that grounds for a *Heter Meia Rabbonim* (permission of 100 rabbis) to circumvent the necessity for a *Get* (Jewish divorce) for the husband?

3. A wife is missing several years. Is that grounds for a *Heter Meia Rabbonim*?

4. A nonreligious man suddenly says his third child, a girl who is 22 years of age, is a *mamzeres* (illegitimate). What is her status?

5. May a *Kohen-Challal* (one who was born of a union between a Cohen and a divorcee) marry a *Giyores* (convert)?

6. A religious man who is considered a *Leivi* is suddenly told by his great aunt that his great grandmother (on his mother's side) was a gentile (implying that he is one too). What is his status?

7. A gentile baby was adopted by a gentile family. He converted at 17. When he reaches 18, he can legally sue to have his adoption records opened to ascertain who his real mother is. Is he obligated to do so; if so, would this create a question of *Shtuki-Asufi* (questionable illegitimacy) if his mother happens to be Jewish?

8. A man who is separated from his wife happened to serve as a witness to a *Get*. He subsequently divorces his wife. May he marry the woman on whose *Get* he signed and witnessed?

9. May a man and woman shake hands?

10. A boy threatened a girl with death if she will not marry him. She consented out of fear. He immediately called over two kosher witnesses and gave her a ring and said, "*Harei At*," etc. Immediately afterwards they appeared before a *Beis Din* (Rabbinic Court) and the *Beis Din* quickly administered a *Get* between the two. This occurrence was not publicized. May this girl now marry a Cohen?

11. May one marry on a particular condition—*Kiddushin Al Tnai*?

12. According to *Halacha* (Jewish law), which of the parents gets child custody after a divorce?

13. A girl suffers from paranoia that some person wishes to kill her. Besides this paranoia she is perfectly normal. Is she considered mentally competent for her marriage to be valid?

14. When saying the text of *Kiddushin* under the *Chuppah*, the man forgot to say with this ring (*Betabas Zu*). Is the *Kiddushin* valid?

15. Does the prohibition of *Yichud* (being alone with the opposite sex) apply to a brother and sister?

16. Does the prohibition of *Yichud* apply in an elevator?

17. Can one be *Mekadesh* with a diamond ring?

18. A *Rav* hears that one of the witnesses he used to a wedding ceremony is a thief. After investigating to his utmost ability he finds that several people who have had dealings with the witness confirm these rumors. However, the witness has an alibi for each occurrence. As much as one is prompted to believe the rumors, there are no actual witnesses to this effect. Does the Rav have to perform a new *Kiddushin*?

19. A woman received a *Get* and subsequently waited the required three months (*Shloish Chodshei Havchona*). She became engaged and made a wedding date. A *Rav* suddenly realizes that her first *Get* had a mistake and quickly administered a new (second) *Get* from her former husband. Is she required to wait three months again?

20. A man who left his wife and fled his country assumes an alias. Which of his names is written when he sends her a *Get*?

21. A couple who were married civilly now request a Rav to perform the proper *halachic* ceremony. However, ashamed of possible publicity, they request that the *Rav* bring along only two witnesses. May the *Rav* do so, as *Birchas Nisuin* needs a *minyan* (quorum of ten)?

22. A couple divorce and then remarry by day. Do they make *Sheva Brochas* at the first meal which is had at night?

23. A husband was jailed for not paying alimony and child support. The wife is ready to waive a partial claim to alimony if he will grant her a *Get*. Is this considered compulsion?

24. Someone whose name is בילא signs ביילע . How is it spelled in a *Kesuba*?

25. During the writing of a *Kesuba,* the *Choson* mistakenly picked up his hat for the שיעבוד נכסים (to commit his possessions) instead of someone else's hat, equivalent to כליו של מקנה instead of כליו של קונה. He realizes his mistake a day later. Do they need a new *Kesuba*?

26. Does a man or woman have the *halachic* right to demand monetary compensation to give or accept a *Get* or is it tantamount to blackmail?

27. A man is seen visiting his former wife unattended. Does that create a new status of marriage?

13. Kollel Bais Avrohom of Los Angeles

The Kollel Bais Avrohom[189] is an example of a relatively new phenomenon that may be expected to grow in the coming years: the community *kolel*. It began initially as part of the outreach program undertaken by Beth Medrash Govoha of Lakewood. The institution has devoted itself to community service and the expansion of Jewish influence in an area previously devoid of such influence. Though most of its students hail from the East Coast and studied in the large *yeshivot* there, its goal is to help them settle in Los Angeles and thus found a community rich in Jewish ideals and values.

The founder of Kollel Bais Avrohom is R. Chaim Fasman, an alumnus of *yeshivot* in Chicago, Israel, and Brooklyn. The *kolel* was opened in

1975 with ten fellows, for the express purpose of bringing an institution of intensive Jewish study to the community of some 400,000 Jews in Los Angeles.

Kolel Structure

Applicants for admission to Kollel Bais Avrohom must be married and have studied at a *kolel* elsewhere for at least five years. They must sit for an interview and oral examination administered by R. Fasman, who serves as *rosh hakolel* and administrator. The applicant must also submit references from former instructors as well as rabbinic authorities familiar with the applicant's work. The student population has ranged from 7 to 12 fellows; in June 1982 there were 11 studying at the *kolel*, between the ages of 26 and 34, slightly older than those at similar institutions, owing to five years of prior study elsewhere.

Upon acceptance into the program, fellows receive stipends of ca. $700 per month. In addition, they are given an annual allowance of ca. $1,000 toward the cost of tuition for their children at local elementary or secondary level *yeshivot*. They also receive travel expenses for two adults to their parents' home, which is usually somewhere on the East Coast. This is in recognition of the sacrifice that residence in Los Angeles represents for most of the students and their families. The *kolel* provides no living accommodations for the students.[190]

The *raison d'être* of the Kollel Bais Avrohom is community influence at entry level. R. Fasman notes the difference between the traditional *"yeshivah kolel"* and a community *kolel* such as his:

> The *yeshivah kolel* looks for young men who can relate to the younger students in the *yeshivah*. The *kolel* is part of the isolated *yeshivah* institution. The community *kolel* seeks to be part of the community. Its efforts are aimed toward community service. The Los Angeles *kolel* was the first such type in the United States.[191]

The *kolel* presence has had a profound influence upon the Jewish community of Los Angeles, apart from its specific outreach programs. The *kolel* has served as a center of worship and study for those who do not count themselves among its students. An elementary level *yeshivah*, Toras Emes, has been established to service the needs of *kolel* families and others of like mind. Toras Emes is subsidized by the *kolel* in the hope that its presence will encourage more young families to join the Jewish community by taking up residence in the local area.

In addition, a series of adult education classes and lectures have attracted local supporters, and *kolel* wives staff *yeshivot* and educational programs for local girls. A Sephardic Studies Program has recently been established as well as a program for prospective newlyweds. *Kolel* families are active in burial societies and participate in other charity or religious functions. Local kosher establishments depend heavily upon the supporters of the *kolel* to maintain their trade. The *kolel* has clearly added an important dimension to Jewish life in Los Angeles.[192]

Program of Study

Fellows of Kollel Bais Avrohom attend sessions or participate in *kolel*-sponsored activities six to seven days each week, from 7:00 A.M. to 10:00 P.M. Upon acceptance the student is required to remain within the *kolel* for at least two years and to enter some facet of community service for at least three years thereafter. This latter facet is unique among the subjects of this study.

The day is divided into several sessions. Prayers begin at 7:00 A.M. and continue until 9:00 A.M. Morning studies follow until 1:30 P.M. There is a break for lunch, and prayers and the afternoon program follow from 4:00 P.M. until 6:00 P.M. The evening is devoted to further study or classes and community activities conducted by *kolel* students. This generally extends until 10:00 P.M.

The curriculum places emphasis upon the study of *Seder Mo'ed*. In particular, fellows must cover the tractates Shabbat, Pesahim, and Sukkah with the various commentaries and codes. They study in *hevrutot* and are periodically required to present a lecture to their peers within the context of a *haburah*. Lectures are offered by the *rosh hakolel* approximately three times each week, and occasional lectures are delivered by visiting rabbinic scholars.

Faculty

The single faculty member and administrator is R. Fasman, who earns about 30 percent more than the *kolel* fellows and is given health benefits. Housing is provided for him as well. The *kolel* confers no degrees, and those students who seek ordination must apply to rabbinic authorities elsewhere. Thus far, all fellows have done so upon graduation.

Students

Students of Kollel Bais Avrohom are typically graduates of major *yeshivot* on the East Coast, notably Beth Medrash Govoha of Lakewood,

New Jersey, and the Mir Yeshiva of Brooklyn, New York. Their primary motivation for coming to Los Angeles appears to be a genuine desire to uplift the level of Jewish learning and observance in the area. Most are expected to remain there upon graduation and take up positions in the rabbinate, education, or communal work.[193]

Kolel families have three to five children. Wives uniformly work outside the home, generally as teachers at local *yeshivot* or preschool programs. Though there appears to be a close and warm interpersonal relationship between the families, given their common goals and objectives, the rigorous *kolel* program leaves little time for informal socializing. This emerges as a point of contention among several wives who, despite their own dedication, feel that the *kolel* schedule is too demanding. They suggest that this may contribute to the *kolel*'s recent difficulties in recruiting new students.[194].

The *kolel* is intensive yet surprisingly noncompetitive. There is considerable respect extended to the *rosh hakolel* both as a scholar and as a pioneering educator who has helped innovate many local programs of adult education and community service. Though not significantly older than many of his students, he serves as a model for their own personal and religious aspirations and professional objectives.[195]

The *kolel* actively encourages its graduates to enter communal service, Jewish education, and the rabbinate upon graduation. Alumni have been placed as faculty members in several local *yeshivot*, and many graduates take up residence within their respective communities. Much of the extensive outreach program undertaken by the *kolel* is also directed towards the placement of students and graduates within local institutions.

Outreach is a fundamental part of the curriculum of the Kollel Bais Avrohom and in many ways distinguishes the community *kolel* from those more directly linked to a large *yeshivah*. *Kolel* fellows offer a variety of adult education courses in topics ranging from elementary Hebrew to advanced Talmud study. In addition, special programs have been organized for recent graduates of *yeshivah* high schools, Jews of Sephardic descent, and newcomers to Jewish life. Every *kolel* fellow is involved in at least one of these programs, and this involvement is given high priority within the curriculum.

The *kolel* also styles itself as a center for Jewish culture and ritual. Many within the community have chosen to join its Sabbath and holiday prayers. Inquiries and referrals regarding aspects of Jewish law and practice have been forwarded to the *rosh hakolel*, and individuals have made use of an informal counseling service developed to encourage greater religious observance.[196]

As noted, many alumni have remained within the local community upon graduation from the *kolel*. There is a regularly published alumni newsletter that keeps them informed of *kolel* activities, and all appear to exhibit a high level of loyalty to the institution. However, given the youth of the *kolel* and the relatively small number of its graduates, alumni have not been able to offer much financial support. Consequently, fund raising, particularly within the local community, has been a major part of R. Fasman's responsibilities.

Accountability

As with many other subjects of this study, accountability at Kollel Bais Avrohom is highly subjective and unsystematic. There are no examinations, nor are attendance and punctuality carefully monitored. No incentives exist to encourage productivity, nor are there penalties for poor performance. Evaluation is purely a function of the informal perceptions of the *rosh hakolel*.

However, with twelve students or less, the *rosh hakolel* claims that he can monitor the progress of his students without formal examinations. In addition, there is some attempt to survey the opinions of participants in adult education or outreach programs given by the individual student. Thus, a composite evaluation of his activities both within the *kolel* and the community emerges. The *rosh hakolel* is also quick to add that careful screening of applicants has allowed him to choose students of high caliber, obviating the need for systematic evaluation.[197]

14. KOLEL YESHIVA GEDOLAH ZICHRON MOSHE

The Kolel Yeshiva Gedolah Zichron Moshe traces its beginnings to Yeshiva Zichron Moshe, an elementary school founded in the Bronx in the early 1950s. Its director, R. Yeruham Gorelick, was a student of R. Israel Meir HaKohen (Hafez Hayyim) and studied at the *yeshivah* of Brisk. In addition to serving as director, he simultaneously held a position as a lecturer in Talmud in the upper division of the Rabbi Isaac Elchanan Theological Seminary of Yeshiva University.

As a result of demographic changes in the western sector of the Bronx where the *yeshivah* was located, the local Jewish community was gradually depleted. By the late 1960s it was no longer possible to maintain the *yeshivah*, and the property was sold. There was never any intention of closing the institution, however, and a grand relocation scheme was undertaken.

Rather than choose a new site within New York City, the *yeshivah* purchased a campus in Sullivan County, in the well-known Catskill Mountains resort area, about 100 miles northwest of the city. The restructured school includes a secondary and undergraduate division as well as an elementary unit, primarily to serve the children of faculty.

The institution was directed by R. Gorelick's two sons, R. Abba and R. Leib, who began the task of fund raising among the local citizenry almost immediately.[198]

In 1976 the *kolel* was added. Although part of the original plan, its dedication was delayed several years to allow for the completion of a large apartment complex intended for *kolel* families, whose rent is subsidized by the *yeshivah*. In addition, the formation of the *kolel* was also, in part, a response to demands from interested persons who foresaw the presence of *kolel* fellows as an important influence upon younger students. Thus, the Yeshiva Zichron Moshe was envisioned as a complete institution of Jewish education. Isolated from the distractions of the "big city" yet not so far as to inhibit student recruitment, it would provide education from early childhood through postgraduate study.[199]

The Kolel Yeshiva Zichron Moshe began with four students in 1976. All were graduates of its lower division and were well known to its faculty and administration. In August 1983 there were eighteen *kolel* fellows. Between 1976 and 1983, only two students applied to the *kolel* from other institutions, thus promoting a certain sense of isolation and intellectual "inbreeding" within the institution.

Kolel Structure

Yeshiva Zichron Moshe is located on a large, rustic campus in Fallsburg, New York. The complex includes a large *bet midrash*, classrooms, a synagogue, dormitories, and apartments surrounding the main building. In addition, there are dining facilities and administrative offices, all of which are available to the *kolel*. The *bet midrash* contains a library of about 1,000 volumes, including collections of Bible commentaries, Talmud, rabbinic studies, and Jewish legal codes.

Application to this *kolel* is an extremely informal process. There are no examinations, oral or written. Applicants do not sit for interviews, nor need they submit letters of reference. As noted, virtually all applicants are graduates of the *yeshivah*'s lower division and are, therefore, well known to the faculty and the administration. Indeed, in some instances they have been invited to apply to the *kolel*.

Upon acceptance, students receive a basic stipend of $80 per week, and an additional $7.50 per week for each child. Students may also apply for federal grants and work-study appointments, raising their monthly income to $500 in many cases. In addition, fellows live in housing subsidized by the *yeshivah*. They pay between $50 and $200 per month for two- or three-bedroom apartments including utilities, which amounts to 25–50 percent of actual cost. Finally, the wives of all *kolel* students work outside the home in clerical or child-care positions or at the elementary division of the *yeshivah*. Thus, the average *kolel* family receives approximately $10,000 per year.[200]

The relationship between the *kolel* and its local community has been generally positive, although there are some overtones of ambivalence. The image of Orthodox Jewry has markedly improved among the general citizenry. It must be recalled that Fallsburg, New York, is in the center of a resort area which is very popular within the Orthodox Jewish community of metropolitan New York. During the summer months, local bungalows, hotels, motels, and camps are filled with families seeking refuge from the city's heat.

Despite the financial benefits of this summer influx, local residents generally viewed these transients, with their strange dress, customs, and demands, as "takers." However, the permanent presence of a *yeshivah* community participating in local programs, volunteering for fire patrol or ambulance duty, and generally exhibiting local pride has done much to dispel such resentment. Indeed, the Sullivan County Department of Public Relations claims that the town of Fallsburg has the lowest rate of antisemitism as a result.[201]

One more ameliorative should be mentioned. Tension between a *yeshivah* or other religious institution and its local community often arises because of the former's tax-exempt status. Local officials and their constituents often feel that the new residents make use of municipal services, but do not return their due. The Yeshiva Zichron Moshe is unique, however, in its insistence that despite eligibility for tax exemption, it will indeed pay local taxes, a fact prominently advertised by a large sign at the school's entrance.

Its relationship with the local rabbinate is somewhat less amiable. There are tensions of a social nature, emanating from the fact that the local Jewish community is composed of older, less traditionally observant members who view the young *kolel* families with some suspicion. Interestingly, although the *yeshivah* has been quick to participate in municipal programs, it has been somewhat more hesitant to integrate itself into the local Jewish community, a fact that only reinforces these tensions.

In addition, the presence of the *yeshivah* has created antagonisms of another sort. For many years there has been a small Jewish day school in the area, supported largely by the local community. Though there are sev-

eral *kolel* wives on its faculty, its standards were not considered sufficiently high by the *kolel* families and *yeshivah* instructors, and their children do
not attend it. Moreover, since Zichron Moshe had begun as an elementary
level *yeshivah* in the Bronx, it was natural for it to establish a similar institution in Sullivan County. Thus, there is some resentment for the competition it engenders and its allegedly elitist attitude.

The *yeshivah* has attempted to overcome some of these difficulties by
reaching out to the local Jewish community and providing educational services not hitherto available. It sponsors a lecture in Jewish thought, directed by *yeshivah* faculty, as well as occasional classes in which *kolel*
fellows participate. In addition, special classes and workshops have been
offered for individuals distant from Jewish observance, and older students
from the local day school have been invited to attend Thursday evening
study sessions in the *bet midrash*. The response, however, has not been
impressive thus far.

Program of Study

The *kolel* of Yeshiva Zichron Moshe sets an initial residence requirement
of three years, according to the *rosh yeshivah*, and successful students are
invited to remain beyond that on a year-by-year basis.[202] The daily
program is composed of three sessions and begins with morning prayers at
7:30 A.M., followed by a voluntary but well-attended workshop in practical Jewish law, *Mishnah Berurah*. The first *seder* begins at 9:45 A.M. and
continues until 1:30 P.M.

During this session, *kolel* fellows are expected to study the same Talmudic selections being covered by the *yeshivah* at large. This implies a heavy
emphasis upon texts chosen from Nashim and Nezikin, sections dealing
with domestic law and torts, respectively, and from which an annual cycle
of tractates has emerged. Fellows study with undergraduates during this
period and offer guidance and direction within the context of the *yeshivah*'s
general curriculum.[203]

The second *seder* begins with afternoon prayers at 3:00 P.M. and continues until 7:00 P.M. Here fellows are permitted to pursue topics of their
own interest as well as individual research. Students who have been with
the *kolel* for at least three years may petition the administration to release
them from their morning obligations so that they may devote themselves
full-time to individual research. By July 1983, five students had received
such permission, reflecting the administration's desire to balance the personal interests of the fellows with the perceived importance of integrating
the *kolel* within the general structure of the *yeshivah*.[204]

Finally, *kolel* fellows are involved with remedial work during their evening hours. In general, this implies study and review with younger students in need of academic support. Though such work is usually performed at the *bet midrash*, a fellow may be granted special permission to have the student visit his home each evening—a practice that the administration appears to discourage. Though fellows generally study in *hevrutah*, a *haburah* has recently been formed to study the tractate Hullin.

R. Leib Gorelick, the *rosh hakolel*, lectures to this group once each week, and members occasionally present their own research. In addition, the entire *yeshivah* attends a lecture by R. Abba Gorelick, the *rosh yeshivah*, every other week, and those studying the same topics as the *yeshivah* generally attend a daily session led by R. Wachtal, who is the Talmud instructor of the senior undergraduate class. Finally, fellows study *musar* daily, thirty minutes before evening prayers; the talk is delivered by the *mashgi'ah* each Wednesday.

The *yeshivah* confers no degrees upon its graduates, operating under the principle that study in a *kolel* should be undertaken for its own sake and should offer no tangible rewards. However, in the evenings several students travel to Monsey, New York, where they study the texts traditionally required for rabbinic ordination with local *roshei yeshivah*. Upon completion, they may sit for the examination and thus earn their ordination privately.[205]

Faculty

The faculty is comprised of R. Abba Gorelick, the *rosh yeshivah*; R. Leib Gorelick, his brother and *rosh hakolel*; plus a Talmud lecturer and a *mashgi'ah*. The faculty members earn $15,000–$20,000 per year and receive a housing subsidy and various medical benefits. Most are graduates of the Brisk Yeshiva of Jerusalem, while instructors in the lower division are alumni of Zichron Moshe.

Students

Fellows of the Kolel Zichron Moshe are all married and between the ages of 24 and 32. All are American-born and alumni of the undergraduate division of Yeshiva Zichron Moshe. In most ways they are similar to students of the other non-*hasidic* subjects of this study. *Kolel* families typically have two or three children. As noted, wives frequently work outside the home to supplement the family income. They generally fill positions as teachers in local elementary *yeshivot*, clerical workers, or babysitters.

Most fellows aspire to positions on the Talmud faculty of advanced *yeshivot*. The administration of the *yeshivah* has recognized that such opportunities are limited. In the words of the *rosh yeshivah*:

> Realistically, the market for such jobs is very slim. Many *kolel* graduates are taking jobs teaching in elementary and high school *yeshivot*. . . . With the numbers increasing in *kolelim*, the difficulties of placing graduates will be ever greater.[206]

The *yeshivah* has responded to this difficulty in two ways. First, the administration claims to be highly selective in admission, thus decreasing the number of those who will enter this market while increasing their quality and competitive edge. In addition, the *yeshivah* has made a small number of positions available to graduates in either instructional or administrative capacities. One suspects that this latter practice will continue and expand, further reinforcing the isolation of this institution.

The atmosphere at the *kolel* is warm yet serious. Although one might expect the limited professional opportunities to heighten competitiveness, this is nowhere apparent. Students maintain a close and confidential relationship with faculty members and their families, underscored by the close living arrangements in this self-contained community.

The *kolel* has produced few alumni thus far. Many have remained within the community and accepted positions at the *yeshivah*. The others have not been motivated either to retain links with the institution or to provide support for its activities. Nevertheless, the *yeshivah* points proudly to the few who have been appointed to the faculty of *yeshivot* in Europe and Israel, correctly noting that they will help expand its reputation as a center for Jewish scholarship in the United States.[207]

Accountability

Monitoring student progress is an informal process at the Kolel Zichron Moshe. There are no examinations, nor does there appear to be any penalty for poor attendance or lateness. Students are offered no rewards for proficiency in their studies, nor are records kept of their accomplishments. However, attendance is monitored by the *mashgi'ah* who may counsel the lagging student.

The *rosh yeshivah* argues that given the small size and structure of the *kolel*, lack of formal accountability does not constitute an impediment to program and achievement:

> The greatest control in an educational institution for higher studies is not the administration but peer pressure. In a small *kolel*, the screening process is

more thorough and the group is close-knit. Everyone knows where each person stands.[208]

Consequently, it has been possible to deal with student weaknesses on an individual basis. A change of study group might be suggested, a different program of study can be arranged, or new responsibilities and opportunities can be scheduled in response to the needs of individual students. Yet, the *rosh yeshivah* concluded, in an unusually frank and sensitive vein: "We deal with lives, families, and reputations. What can be done if one cannot accomplish?"[209] His observation reflects at once the strength and the weakness of the institution.

PART THREE
Analysis of Data

Having described the various subjects of this study, their histories, philosophies, and structures, it is now appropriate to attempt some form of summary analysis based on the data collected. The evaluation of the quantitative data was based in part on informational questionnaires that were completed for each institution; these are complemented by the author's observations. Two statistical techniques, correlation and cross-tabulation, have been used to analyze the data collected.[1]

Correlation is normally employed when both variables are characterized by a "physical unit of measurement which can be agreed upon as a common standard and which is replicable."[2] For purposes of such correlation, eleven variables emerged in the present study, and the correlative table is included in the Appendix (see Table 4). The variables that emerged are (1) length of program in years; (2) hours required per day; (3) age of the faculty; (4) faculty salaries; (5) student income per month; (6) average number of children per student; (7) age of the institution; (8) number of books in the library; (9) original size of the student population; (10) present size of the student population; and (11) mean age of the present student population.

The cross-tabular material includes, *inter alia*, the following qualitative classifications: the type of institution (Lithuanian, *hasidic*, etc.); the presence of a marriage requirement; the administration of formal examinations for purposes of accountability; the existence of outreach programs; and student career goals. Tables 5 and 6 (see Appendix) are constructed to demonstrate differences between samples in a specific variable. Such qualitative analysis is common in the evaluation of nominal data.[3]

In analyzing correlative data, it should be recalled that the presence of a substantial correlation does not necessarily reflect a real association between the two variables, nor does it suggest that one causes the other. Prudence dictates the need for caution in interpreting statistical results, and observation and personal evaluation, where possible, are useful in interpreting such data.

Several descriptions of our subjects appear to emerge, descriptions that may possibly be generalized to institutions not included in this study. For example, when discussing the age of the institution, it is necessary to know that for a variety of historical reasons, the Lithuanian *kolelim* tend to be considerably older than their counterparts. Ordinarily, one might expect such institutions to be better established and, therefore, willing and able to pay their faculty better, offer more student benefits, and retain a more mature student population (with larger families) and an older faculty.

The data confirm some of these assumptions but not all. Older institutions do tend to have older faculties, but do not appear to pay their teachers differently from younger *kolelim*. Indeed, they offer their students lower incomes, yet manage to attract a large number of students who are somewhat younger than those in newer schools and who have considerably smaller families.

Thus, it appears that older *kolelim* are able to retain their faculty and attract students without offering larger material rewards. The fact that their student bodies are younger suggests that this trend will continue for the immediate future. Apparently, attraction to a *kolel* is based on other, less tangible rewards that cannot be easily quantified.

A possible factor may be the reputation of the institution and its faculty. Clearly, this reputation has been earned with time. Furthermore, it may well be that young men who are qualified to enter prestigious *kolelim* can more easily persuade family and in-laws to support their endeavors. Equally, the administrators and staff of such schools can be of great help in exploiting sources of outside income, obviating the necessity for large stipends.

One should also consider that the older institutions can draw from a larger potential student body. As noted, *hasidic kolelim* are of more recent vintage, as are the "community" institutions. These tend to draw upon a very limited pool of students from a particular community or from disciples of the *hasidic* dynasty.

In addition, several older *kolelim* have become somewhat less restrictive in their entrance requirements. Notably the Beth Medrash Govoha, Hafez Hayyim, and Yeshiva University have accepted unmarried fellows into their *kolel* programs. Quite obviously this expands the potential pool of applicants. It also tends to explain why these older institutions have younger students with fewer children.

The issues of attraction and prestige can be joined more directly by examining the relationship between the size of the student populations and several other variables often believed to be related to it. The results are interesting. Academic institutions often believe that they will attract students by reducing the length or intensity of the academic program. Clearly, this is not the case here. There is no relationship between the size of the student body and the number of hours in the academic day.

Equally, it is often thought that a more successful recruitment effort may be waged by increasing research facilities or engaging younger faculty able to better understand the needs of students. These, too, emerge as irrelevant in our sample. The size of the student population relates neither to the number of books in the *kolel* library nor to the age of the faculty.

Finally, reflecting the analysis offered above, the students are not attracted by material benefits or by a well-paid academic staff. Indeed, these two variables correlate negatively, suggesting that the most popular institutions pay less to faculty and students alike. Perhaps because they are most in demand, they compensate with prestige and quality. Clearly, the only marked correlation of note exits between the size of the student body and the age of the institution.

It must be recalled, of course, that the age of the institution is not precisely associated with any of the qualitative categories that have been created for purposes of this study. Notably, the Chabad Kolel, eldest among those in the *hasidic* group, was established in 1960, whereas the *kolel* at Yeshiva University is 32 years old, though its present programs are much newer. Nevertheless, these two *kolelim* can easily be included among those institutions that are better established not only in terms of age but in status and prestige, thus supporting the general conclusion that such criteria are far more important than the material inducements available. Apparently, one who chooses a *kolel* education does not expect a high standard of material well-being provided by the *kolel*. His choices are predicated on other priorities.

The salience of the four typologies developed can be more directly tested by the cross-tabulation of simple means and percentages. Cross-tabulation also provides a valuable summary to illustrate the growth of the *kolel* in America and the factors that characterize that growth. In general, such an analysis also tends to confirm the tentative conclusions reached on the basis of the correlations discussed above.

Table 1. Growth of Kolel in America, By Kolel Type

Category	Mean Age	Student Population at Founding	Student Population 1982–83	Growth, %	Mean % Annual Growth*
Lithuanian (N=5)	34.4	74	711	960.8	27.9
Hasidic (N=4)	14.5	50	200	400	27.6
New (N=4)	16	23	73	317.3	19.8
Community (N=2)	3.5	14	28	200	57.1

Source: Administrative documents provided by each institution.

*Percentage growth divided by mean age.

Table 1 displays some of these data. As noted, the Lithuanian *kolelim* emerge by far as the oldest of the four groups, and the community *kolelim* are of very recent vintage, reflecting the novelty of this approach to Jewish life. It is also interesting to note that the "new" *kolelim* may be new but they are not young. This is a function of the presence of Yeshiva University and of the fact that "new" is here being defined not in regard to age, but in regard to some unique orientation introduced in traditional *kolel* study. Finally, the *hasidic* institutions emerge among the youngest, reflecting the fact that *kolel* study has not been characteristic of these communities.

Also interesting are the data concerning the growth of these institutions, indicated by the increases in their student populations. The total number of students enrolled in these institutions at their founding was only 161. In December 1983, the total student population was 1,012, an increase of 628.6 percent. These figures, extrapolated from the data presented, clearly illustrate the vitality of the *kolel* over the past generation.

In addition, it appears that this growth is closely related to the age of the group, as noted above. Thus, the Lithuanian *kolelim* have increased two-, three-, and fourfold over their respective cohorts. However, these data may be somewhat deceptive, in that the age of the *kolel* may intercede in the analysis.

The final column calculates the mean percentage of annual growth for each group, thus holding age in control. The results are revealing. When removing age as a variable, it appears that the Lithuanian *kolelim* have not experienced a proportionately higher rate of growth than have the *hasidic kolelim* (27.9% vs. 27.6%). Indeed, the most impressive rate of growth—though small in absolute terms—has occurred in the community *kolelim*, 57.1%.

This may reflect two complementary phenomena. It may indicate that the community *kolel* is an idea whose "time has come." For many, the opportunity to study at a large prestigious institution may not be realistic, whereas study at a local *kolel* is more attractive. Furthermore, there may be a group of students who feel a mission to bring their work to the community and thereby fulfill more than a purely academic function.

Second, the community *kolelim* may have come on the scene at a time when American Jewish society is more receptive to *kolel* study than in the past. The path having been blazed by the older institutions, these new *kolelim* are reaping the benefits of seeds sown elsewhere. In this formulation, one might expect continued growth among all *kolelim* and a slower rate of growth among the community institutions after an initial lunge into the marketplace. It must be recalled that these data are based on only two such institutions, and evaluations should be offered with the utmost caution. Clearly, further study of the community *kolel* is needed.

The data also yield some interesting inferences regarding the nature of the student body that has chosen *kolel* education. Table 2 presents these findings, grouping them once more according to *kolel* type. The Lithuanian *kolelim* have a much larger mean student population than any other group, indeed ten times larger than the community *kolelim*. Of course, these calculations are somewhat unfairly influenced by the presence of the Beth Medrash Govoha in the Lithuanian group, which has 474 students. In addition, the relatively small size of the community *kolel* may also contribute to its popularity, although continued growth will soon mitigate this effect.

Table 2. Kolel Student By Kolel Type

Category	Mean Student Population	Mean Student Age	Marriage Required, %	Mean No. Children per Student
Lithuanian (N = 5)	142.2	28.2	60	2.9
Hasidic (N = 4)	50	27.5	100	3.25
New (N = 3)	24.3	29.9	66.7	2.7
Community (N = 2)	14	29	100	3.5

Source: Administrative documents provided by each institution, interviews, and observations.

It appears that students within each group of *kolelim* are approximately the same age, with those of the *hasidic* schools somewhat younger. There also appear to be differences in the size of their families: the community *kolelim* are highest, followed by the *hasidic* group.

As noted above, not all *kolelim* require an applicant to be married upon entering the program. Predictably, those with the largest number of children per student require marriage at entry, whereas those groups that do not require marriage at entry exhibit smaller family sizes. Thus, the data may be contaminated by the presence of singles or others who married during their tenure at the institution. These will doubtless have smaller families than those in institutions that require all students to be married before they can be accepted.

Finally, the data can be manipulated to offer some insight into the differences of programs among the various groups. Table 3 presents these data in regard to the mean age of the faculty and the percentage of *kolelim* within each group that requires students to study in *haburot*, participate in outreach programs, and take some form of objective examinations. Once more, tentative inference is possible.

Table 3. Structure of Kolel Program By Kolel Type

Category	Mean Age of Faculty	Percentage with Haburot*	Administers Written Exams, %	Outreach Programs, %
Lithuanian (*N* = 5)	51	60	0	80
Hasidic (*N* = 4)	30	25	50†	25
New (*N* = 3)	36.7	33.3	66.7	33.3
Community (*N* = 2)	40	50	0	100

Source: Administrative documents provided by each institution, interviews, and observations.

*In all cases, *haburot* are employed along with *hevrutot*.

†Written examinations voluntary.

A brief glance at the first column is instructive. Not only are the Lithuanian *kolelim* older as institutions, but their faculty members are substantially older. As noted earlier, rather than being a disadvantage, this may well be an attraction. Conversely, the relative youth of the faculty members at the new *kolelim* and particularly among the *hasidic* schools is striking. When one recalls that the average age of their students is just under 30, it is clear that these faculty members are contemporaries of their charges, just barely older than the students themselves, and are probably graduates from the same program or a similar one elsewhere.

There also appear to be important differences in the manner by which study is organized. Table 3 presents the percentage of each group that requires *haburah* study in conjunction with *hevrutah* work. It appears that the majority of Lithuanian *kolelim* do encourage *haburot*. Clearly, this is an extra effort for students, who must prepare and present their work before groups of peers. Ostensibly it is a form of evaluation for students, offering them valuable experience for later careers in education or the rabbinate.

This is followed closely by the community *kolelim*, as might be expected. These new institutions were founded through the efforts of older institutions, maintain close affiliations with them, and recruit from within their ranks. It is to be expected that the academic formats would be similar. It might also be added that those community *kolelim* which do not employ *haburot* regularly, do employ them periodically, though this was not recorded in the present data.

Such methodology appears to be foreign to the *hasidic* or new *kolelim;* that generally encourage students to work in small groups. Particularly in the case of the *hasidic kolelim*, this may reflect their general inexperience with *kolel* study or the lack of a strong tradition therein. Thus, the question of whether the *haburah* is a useful vehicle remains open. Its use among Lithuanian institutions is less a matter of rational choice than historical circumstance. Not being part of those circumstances—indeed not being in the mainstream of *kolel* study at all—all *hasidic* institutions have not generally chosen to move in this direction. The same may be applied to the new *kolelim*, though with somewhat less rigor.

A glance at the data regarding written examinations may also prove instructive. Here the differences are equally striking. None of the Lithuanian *kolelim* or the fast-growing community institutions that they have spawned require such examinations. By contrast, half the *hasidic* schools and the majority of those in the new group have such examinations. It must be noted, however, that while examinations are required among the majority of new *kolelim*, they are voluntary among half the *hasidic* schools.

Nonetheless, the implications are intriguing. Despite the stereotypical demand for academic excellence and erudition among Lithuanian schools, no examinations are offered. By contrast, the frequent claim that academic performance is not a traditional part of the *hasidic* heritage is contradicted by the presence of examinations, voluntary though they may be.

More cynically, might it be that at least a part of the success of the Lithuanian schools, aside from their vintage and the venerable nature of their faculties, is the absence of objective accountability? Here a student might choose a prestigious institution with all the attendant community status, study at the feet of a renowned scholar, work in consort with like-minded fellows, and rarely be held formally accountable.

Of course, the point should not be made too sharply. Each institution insists that despite the absence of formal examinations, accountability is maintained through the regular contact of student and teacher plus the impact of peer pressure in *haburot* and *hevrutot*. Indeed, this may be the case among those institutions possessing 30 or 40 students. However, at the Beth Medrash Govoha, which has nearly 500 fellows, or at the Mir Central Institute, which has 119, one is hard-pressed to accept this proposition uncritically.

The small size of the new *kolelim* certainly facilitates accountability. The majority administer examinations and require them of their fellows. In large measure, this is what makes these schools "new" and, as the data illustrate, this represents a substantial departure from traditional practice, especially among well-established and prestigious *kolelim*.

Finally, the data in regard to outreach programs may also allow some inference. As might be expected, *hasidic* institutions tend to be insular. Their primary mandate is service to their immediate communities, and *kolel* fellows here do not aspire to outward mobility. They hope to find a place for themselves within the community and become loyal followers of the particular *rebbe*. The exception is Chabad, for whom outreach is in the very fiber of its ideology. The hope is still to fulfill the *rebbe*'s wishes, but the nature of his wishes differs from those of his colleagues elsewhere.

Similarly, outreach tends not to be characteristic of the new *kolelim*. Among the elements of their novelty are strict academic procedure and a powerful commitment to performance and accountability. Important though outreach may be, it is not seen as part of their mission. Rather, it is their role to serve as a research arm for the Jewish community, fulfilling the great *mitzvah* of Torah study and placing their considerable academic facilities at the disposal of those in need.

The exception here is Yeshiva University. Though there is a similar commitment to academic performance and accountability through objective examination, the institution considers outreach a vital aspect of its program. In addition, its students tend to be far less insular than their counterparts, since a college education is a prerequisite to their acceptance in the *kolel* program. Finally, one cannot discount the fact that the *kolel* is but a small part of a large university structure, which virtually ensures a broader world view among its fellows. Indeed, these are precisely the factors that governed its inclusion in the "new" category.

What is somewhat unexpected is the outreach score of the Lithuanian group. Stereotypically, the large and established *kolelim* are seen as creating a society unto themselves with little regard for the needs of the broader Jewish community. This view is at odds with the results of this study. Fully 80 percent of the Lithuanian *kolelim* analyzed here maintain active outreach programs, performing an important social and spiritual service for those on the periphery of Jewish life. This is an important difference between the Lithuanian institutions and most others.

The tendency is yet further reflected among the community *kolelim*. Indeed, in some ways the very initiation of these establishments is a tribute to the outreach programs of their Lithuanian predecessors. Many members of the faculty and administrators in the community *kolelim* are graduates of Lithuanian institutions and may well have begun their careers doing community outreach work there. The primary mission of the community *kolel* is public service—from which the category title was chosen—and it is not surprising that both of those studied here maintain programs of outreach to the general Jewish community.

A few brief words of summary are in order. This section has sought to examine some of the quantitative implications that emerge from this study of the *kolel* and its influence upon American Jewish life in contemporary times. It should be seen as just one small part of the general analysis, and any conclusions reached are tentative and suggestive at best.

Yet several inferences emerge. In the first instance, the growth of the *kolel* as a form of postgraduate study has been impressive. Measured in terms of the number of students now attending these programs, as compared to their original size, the *kolelim* cited have increased over ninefold.

Nevertheless, one should not overestimate the importance of this form of study, based on its proportional growth alone. These students still represent a tiny minority even among Orthodox Jews. For many outside this narrow camp, *kolel* study is viewed with indifference or antagonism. Consequently, the various outreach programs that have been undertaken are as valuable to the institution as they may be to the various communities they serve.

It is also important to emphasize the characteristics of *kolelim* that emerge as most attractive to students (measured by the size of their student body). Though critics may claim that *kolel* students are not productive members of society, and that their work is supported by public till or familial largess, it appears that material comfort has little to do with the appeal of a particular *kolel*. The data presented here suggest that such variables as size, monthly stipend, length of the program or of the daily sessions, faculty salary, or size of the library do not correlate positively with size of the student body.

Indeed, the single factor that exhibits a marked relationship with the size of the student body is the age of the institution. Apparently, applicants are attracted to the larger, well-established, and prestigious *kolelim*, even though these tend to offer fewer material benefits and have older faculties. Indeed, perhaps precisely because the newer institutions have not yet attained these levels of prestige, they are required to offer larger stipends.

As for the nature of the student body, it has been demonstrated that students of *hasidic kolelim* tend to be somewhat younger than others, while those in the community institutions appear to have larger families.

Certain differences are equally evident in examining the structure of the programs within each category. The Lithuanian institutions and their community cohorts are most likely to require students to participate in *haburah* sessions. Similarly, these two groups are far more likely to incorporate outreach programs in their curriculum. That the two groups should have similar programs is not surprising, since in many ways the Lithuanian *kolelim* spawned those in the community group and strong affiliations are still maintained between the two.

Finally, these two groups stand apart from others in their decision not to administer objective examinations for purposes of student evaluation and performance appraisal. It is claimed that the *haburah* as an educational form and the intimacy of the *kolel* structure provide ample means of accountability. In particular, the new *kolelim* have rejected this claim. They have made strict accountability and a commitment to objective evaluation a hallmark of their programs, in some instances attaching monetary incentives to performance.

Indeed, one must be skeptical about the value of informal and subjective evaluation, particularly in the larger and better established institutions. The close, personal student-faculty relationships that may have characterized American *kolelim* at an earlier time are no longer uniformly true, particularly among those institutions that are the most popular. The dependence upon subjective appraisals and peer influence alone may well be illusory.

PART FOUR
Summary Observations

It should be noted that the *kolel* in the United States has transcended what may have originally been a purely educational function and has become an important part of the social environment of Orthodoxy. The reasons for this are many. To begin, one cannot overestimate the importance of the Holocaust, for it was this horrible tragedy that provided much of the impetus for the development of *kolel* institutions on American soil.

Aside from the overwhelming tragedy that befell the Jewish community generally, the Holocaust wreaked particular havoc upon Jewish intellectual life. Countless numbers of great scholars perished in the onslaught, along with their students and supporters. Schools and educational institutions, operative for generations, were shut down, their faculties either destroyed or forced to take their students into various forms of exile. The disruptions and discontinuities that resulted are impossible to detail, and many wondered whether the rich religious scholarship of East European Jewry could ever be reproduced elsewhere.

A small number of leading European scholars were able to survive the tragedy by seeking refuge in the United States or in Israel just prior to the war. Others found safe harbor as temporary refugees elsewhere—the Orient, for example—with the intention of settling in the United States afterward. Though several of the *kolelim* were established as *yeshivot* earlier, it was the arrival of these remaining scholars and their students that marked a turning point in the history of the *kolel* in the United States.

Scholars such as R. Kotler and R. Kalmanowitz were much dismayed by what they found upon their arrival in the United States. In many ways, it was necessary for them to start virtually from the beginning in recruiting students, persuading supporters, and making a place for their institutions. America appeared to be a society that was not generally favorable to the kind of study the *kolel* prescribed for the married student, that is, full-time devotion to Torah, with the family supported by the wife's part-time labor, the benevolence of parents, and the "public dole."

Nevertheless, the founders and leaders of these institutions felt a very special mission. It was left to them to create a monument, as it were, to those who had fallen. They would not allow the Nazi scheme to succeed, in the sense of obliterating Jewish culture through terror. The *kolel* in America was to stand as an example of how a new generation could take over from those who had been brutally uprooted, and keep the flame of their accomplishments brightly lit.

Though it complicated their task, the mission was the more keenly felt because of the nature of American society. American society, far more open and mobile than that of Europe, had generally welcomed the Jewish community and encouraged a high degree of political, social and economic integration. Though this was highly appreciated by most American Jews, the newly arrived *roshei yeshivah* viewed it with alarm. To them it spelled the possible demise of authentic Jewish life through ignorance, assimilation, and antipathy to traditional patterns of authority. The challenge of the *kolel* was, therefore, not just to ensure the memory of the past but to affirm and structure the future.

As a result, the *kolel* of today may be seen as a form of "pressure group" in Orthodox Jewish society. Its leaders, particularly though not exclusively those of the Lithuanian typology, perceive their students as models of proper Jewish life and as a priority for the survival of the Jewish community. Constantly demanding more stringent standards of observance, education, and support, these *kolel* leaders have won some acceptance in Orthodox circles. Indeed, it is an acceptance only partially reflected by the considerable growth of their institutions in terms of student body and financial support.

In addition, the concept of the *kolel* appears to have undergone some change. The *kolel* of nineteenth-century Europe was generally reserved for a small group of exceptional students who would be groomed for specific religious positions or academic or communal distinction. Though that ideal still exists, the aspiration to *kolel* study is no longer so clearly restricted. Increasingly, several years of familial support for *kolel* study has become a prenuptial requirement, even for those not known for their outstanding scholarship.

Perhaps the best examples of such development are the Beth Medrash Govoha of Lakewood and the Mirrer Yeshiva Central Institute. There, hundreds of students, at a variety of academic levels, study very much independently, and few formal or systematic procedures are used to evaluate progress or performance. Indeed, both personal observation and informal interviews have confirmed that there are many among these students whose work is known to be inferior.

Moreover, by no means is the modern *kolel* exclusively a training ground for Jewish rabbinic or academic leadership. Particularly in these larger and more prestigious institutions, there are many students who fully intend to enter the world of business or the professions and who may even scoff at those who seek a career in education or communal service. Their decision to study at the *kolel* may be related to a genuine desire to study Torah full-time before the pressures of employment preclude it. It may also be related to motivations of prestige or trend in an enclosed subculture, which often pays a premium for bridegrooms seeking this course of action.

In addition, the *kolel* as a social and educational form has also taken root in Jewish communities whose European antecedents lacked such a tradition. This work cites four *kolelim* affiliated with *hasidic* communities, none of whom supported such institutions prior to their establishment in the United States over the past two decades. Consequently, leaders of these *kolelim* uniformly bemoan the difficulties they experience in convincing their communities that such an endeavor is worthy of their support, despite the fact that their fathers did not found *kolelim* in Europe. Ironically, while the Lithuanian *kolelim* are busy convincing their supporters that European traditions can be re-created on these shores, the *hasidic kolel* leaders are arguing that "America is different."

It should not be construed, however, that the *hasidic kolelim* have simply reproduced the Lithuanian prototype. Clearly, the *hasidic kolelim* reflect the unique needs and social environments within which they were spawned, and there appear to be important differences among them.

In regard to curriculum, the Lithuanian institutions tend to emphasize a sequence of Talmudic study with little regard to its immediate relevance or practical value. Tractates dealing with civil and criminal codes, domestic law, and holiday ritual are given equal weight on a rotating basis. Students are generally expected to keep pace with the larger *yeshivah* while pursuing their own research and independent study.

Of somewhat secondary importance are the various codes of law which serve as the basis for applied Jewish practice. Some attention is also paid to the study of Jewish ethics. While this was a far more important part of the curriculum among the European antecedents of these institutions, it is given barely passing notice today. In most cases, attendance at a *musar shmues* is either loosely monitored or formally voluntary. Students are frequently permitted to replace it with other study or outreach work.

The *hasidic kolelim* emphasize *sugyot*, topical studies, rather than mastery of large portions of text. Practical *halakhah* is the focus, and study begins with the codes and proceeds from there. The graduate of a *hasidic kolel* may lack the erudition and broad scholarship of his Lithuanian counterpart, but he will be far better prepared to serve as a mediator and judge of Jewish ritual within his community or one similar to it.

In many ways, this is as it must be. Outstanding students at Lithuanian institutions aspire to follow in the footsteps of their teachers and mentors. Rather than serve the community directly outside the institution, they hope to enter the academic world and make their mark as the scholars and instructors of the next generation. Nor do they care to instruct the uninitiated or the very young. In its pristine form, their hope is to teach at the same postgraduate level in which they presently find themselves.

A student at a *hasidic kolel* does not aspire to be a *rosh hakolel*, by and large. His position is far less well established in the community and, in many cases, he came by it as a result of his familial relationship to the *rebbe*, the community's spiritual head. A *rosh hakolel* in the *hasidic* community is likely to be only a few years older than his students and may not necessarily be regarded as a major scholar.

Rather, these fellows aspire to positions of communal service as rabbis, teachers, and practicing mediators of the law. Indeed, in some instances they are preparing themselves for some particular mission that will be chosen by the *rebbe* or one of his associates. In an environment not yet fully receptive to the presence of and need for a community-supported *kolel*, the importance of producing graduates who can offer practical service and perform tangible functions is self-evident.

In addition to these areas of study, *hasidic* institutions also have dedicated themselves to preserving the unique aspects of their community and history. Thus, while Lithuanian *kolelim* give at least some attention to *musar* as a secondary unit of study, *hasidic* schools provide for much more extensive analyses of *hasidic* philosophy and of the works of the present *rebbe* or his ancestors. In the case of Chabad, the redaction and organization of *hasidic* works has become a major research project assigned to leading students of the *kolel*.

It should be noted that there are important exceptions to these general differences between *hasidic* and Lithuanian *kolelim*. The Beth Medrash Govoha of Lakewood, for example, has succeeded in attracting a large and varied student body, expanding from its original class of 12 in 1945 to almost 500 in 1985. As a result, it has made inroads into several communities and counts among its students many who are of distinctly *hasidic* background. Consequently, programs and courses of study relating to *hasidic* philosophy and ritual practice are now offered there in lieu of the study of *musar*. Doubtless no such courses were available at its parent institutions in Europe in the past century.

Conversely, the Kolel of Zanz, affiliated with the *hasidic* community led by the *Rebbe* of Zanz in Union City, New Jersey, has adapted a curriculum and method of study clearly at variance with the generalizations offered earlier. Emphasis is placed upon the study of the entire Talmud with little regard for the practicality of one or another section. Strict accountability is the rule, and students sit for written examinations regularly. Progress and performance are rewarded materially and in direct proportion to quality. In this sense, the Zanz Kolel has followed the lead of the Mechon Hahoyroa, one of the "new" *kolelim* analyzed in this study.

Aside from these two major subdivisons among *kolelim*, two other types were defined for purposes of analysis and explanation. These were the community institutions and the "new" *kolelim*. However, unlike the others, these two were not natural subdivisions and their development as typologies was not without attendant difficulties. The matter deserves some brief discussion.

The community *kolel* is very much an American invention and a very recent one at that. The two discussed here, Kollel Bais Avrohom of Los Angeles and Kolel Zichron Moshe of Fallsburg, New York, have been chosen as prototypes, representing institutions that have emerged all over the United States during the past decade. The mark of the community *kolel* is its comprehensive program of outreach and community service.

These institutions are still quite small, not very well known, and very much dependent upon the better established Lithuanian *kolelim*. They must lean for continued support upon local communities, to which their approach to Judaism is foreign at best. The prognosis for their funding, student recruitment, and faculty status are all unclear. Yet it should be recalled that they exhibit the greatest annual growth rate of all groups under discussion here.

Most problematic was the group termed "new" *kolelim*. These were joined together, not because they had common elements, but because they were each significantly different from all others studied. They were defined as "new" because they introduced a new element to *kolel* study, although this might be claimed by the community institutions as well. Among themselves, the three members of this group—Yeshiva University, Kollel Horabanim, and Mechon Hahoyroa—differed in terms of curricula, emphasis, faculty, and student body.

Committed to producing Judaic scholars with strong credentials in areas of secular study, Yeshiva University requires a university degree of all who apply for *kolel* entrance. It is an institution that has long styled itself among the "modern" elements of American Orthodoxy, willing to confront American culture and assimilate many aspects of its dress, style, and thought. Much of this is anathema to other institutions under discussion. Nevertheless, in regard to its curriculum, areas of concentration, method, and program, the *kolel* at Yeshiva University fits easily into the Lithuanian model, though its emphasis upon outreach approaches that of the community *kolel*. Although outreach is not part of the *kolel*, the fellows do participate in such activities. The program of the Kolel Elyon has recently projected a series of community lectures presented by the *kolel* students. The goal of the Chaver Kolel at Yeshiva University is to develop a knowledgeable or professional person who will be a learned Jew.

By contrast, the Mechon Hahoyroa places emphasis solely upon the intensive study of Talmud and Codes, to the exclusion of any other form of knowledge or activity. No time is allocated for outreach programs and certainly no secular study would be permitted. What is unique about this institution is its sophisticated system of written examinations, linked to the fellow's stipend. The program has been introduced at the Zanz Kolel, as noted, and is very much the outgrowth of the values and support of one individual, R. Azriel Tauber. Many of its results are impressive.

Finally, the Kollel Horabonim is chiefly a research institute which meets for only a few hours each night. It dedicates itself to questions and inquiries directed by rabbis or community leaders and sees itself primarily as a service organization for the Jewish community. Indeed, its name, the "Rabbis' Kolel," derives from the fact that all its fellows have studied and been ordained elsewhere, and many continue their work at other *kolelim* during the day, "learning-for-pay" at this institution to supplement their other stipends.

As should be evident, this group of *kolelim* is heterogeneous and linked together only by the very unique factors that separated its members from others under discussion. Consequently, any conclusions presented, whether qualitative or quantitative, must be regarded as highly tentative and exploratory.

In reviewing the data, this writer was left with a sense of concern and pessimism regarding several specific aspects of *kolel* study in the United States. Of great concern are the aspirations of those who study in the *kolel* and the honesty with which such aspirations are treated by the institution. Also disturbing is the pattern of future support for *kolel* study by those sectors of the Jewish public that should be its natural constituency. Finally, the general lack of systematic evaluation to hold students accountable for their progress presents similar concerns.

As noted, many students within the *kolel*—particularly those in the Lithuanian institutions and the community *kolelim*—have chosen their *roshei yeshivah* as the models for their own aspirations. When asked about career choices, most of these express the desire to enter Jewish education at the highest level. Yet it is clear that there simply will not be a sufficient number of such positions available. Those that do become vacant will not likely be awarded to a newly graduated *kolel* fellow.

At best, many of these students will enter Jewish education at the primary or secondary levels or serve in other communal areas, awaiting their turn at the positions they covet. When confronted with this reality, students frequently claim that the growth of the *kolel* today implies the need for many more outstanding professors of Talmud in the future. When pressed further, most simply proclaim their faith in the Lord, for He will provide.

That the values and hopes of these students tend to be highly idealistic and not matched by reality is not disturbing in itself. The idealism is typical of those still undergoing their training, and it is common among many in various fields. What is more disconcerting, however, is the fact that the institutions are doing little to prepare their fellows for the realities that they well know await them. Rather than offering alternatives, they tend to further insulate the student, encouraging him to believe that there will be a place for him on the faculty of a *bet midrash* or postgraduate program.

RECOMMENDATIONS AND SUGGESTIONS

Kolel institutions would be well served if they embarked on certain kinds of training programs for their students in various areas of management, industry, or in secondary and elementary education. While a full-scale curriculum would be obtrusive and unnecessary, the *kolel* and *yeshivah* could likely legitimate such alternatives by making counseling, guidance, and training available as part of their regular program. Indeed, they might thereby open up new areas of recruitment for students who do not foresee a career in Jewish education, yet who would like to continue their Torah studies without injuring their chances in a limited job market. Such programs might also create new supporters among graduates who enter the world of business and commerce, yet retain loyalties to their alma mater.

The point fits neatly with another concern, support for *kolel* study. Data collected here indicate that the mean stipend for a *kolel* family is $750 per month, with several of the larger *kolelim* offering well below that figure. Clearly, even a student family with a working wife must constantly seek other sources of support. Often, this is provided by parents, although such funds are by no means limitless, especially as the family grows and the student decides to remain in the program beyond the first few years.

Consequently, institutions encourage their fellows to seek government funds through welfare programs, food stamps, educational grants, and the like. Over 50 percent of those institutions studied here indicated that this is their common practice. One must question the wisdom of such activities.

In the first instance, support from public sources tends to be somewhat precarious. Particularly under the Reagan Administration, many an institution of higher learning has found that the Federal Government cannot be automatically assumed to shoulder the burden of tuition and student support. Such largess has been anathema for past generations of Jewish scholars, and encouraging the Jewish community to seek government support for Torah study at the highest level raises serious qualms.

Issues arising out of investigations and audits often accompany broad government support. Mistakes are common human occurrences. Should Jewish educational institutions not be concerned that government funds have usually resulted in involvement in the programs, curricula, and admissions policies?

The issue is exacerbated by a second element. Much has been made of the *kolel* as an example of the relationship between Issachar and Zebulun, i.e., the partnership between the scholar and the layman. The latter financially supports the former, and the resulting study is to the credit of both. However, the *kolel* has yet to make a sufficiently profound impact on the broader Jewish community, even though its own graduates hope to send their children to similar institutions in the future. The obvious problem arises from this proliferation of Issachars, willing to continue study, and the constant dearth of Zebuluns who see the value in its support. Will there be sufficient interest in the future to keep the partnership alive?

One important response has already been attempted. The *kolelim* can best serve their own needs as well as those of the Jewish community by developing aggressive programs of outreach. Aside from the obvious benefits which would accrue to the Jewish community in the form of education programs, counseling, holiday celebrations, and the like, such an undertaking might help to alleviate the difficulties outlined above.

Outreach would help the *kolelim* make a case for their importance in

Jewish life. It would likely serve an important public-relations function, increasing the visibility of the institutions, winning friends, allies, and advocates. New opportunities for fund raising would be made available, and the wall of suspicion and mistrust that often envelops the *kolel* would be weakened and reduced.

Furthermore, the development of social networks through programs of outreach might help create or make available employment for *kolel* graduates. Rabbinic, administrative, or communal positions not otherwise open to these students, could become available as a natural result of the greater contact and respect that would emerge. Those placed would then help to further the status of the *kolel* and win new allies to its cause.

In many ways, such a plan has already been undertaken by community *kolelim*, by the fellows of the Chabad Kolel, and by those of Yeshiva University. The Lithuanian *kolelim* have followed, albeit haltingly. They can be expected to continue on this route as it becomes evident that the survival of the institution may well depend upon how it is perceived by a broader segment of the Jewish public. Overcoming this problem of "image" may also open the door to greater support from nondenominational Jewish organizations, such as the United Jewish Appeal, the Federation of Jewish Philanthropies, or the American Jewish Committee.

Along with an attempt to expand the influence of the *kolel*, a reduction in the size and number of the institutions themselves should be considered. Although the *kolel* is a European invention, the idea that large numbers of students are entitled to such study is clearly an American variation. Perhaps reserving the *kolel* only for those very outstanding graduates of lower division *yeshivot* would reduce the number of fellows in need of support and make it easier to justify appeals for funds. Alternatively, those who are not ranked as outstanding could be left to seek their own support privately. Only those most deserving, by dint of ability and merit, would receive stipends, housing, and other benefits. Surely there is ample precedent for such a decision.

Another facet of the *kolel*'s visibility and image relates to the general absence of systematic evaluation of student work and the common impression that there is little accountability within the walls of the institution. Without doubt, it will be difficult to convince a new generation of supporters, or to reach out to those on the fringe of Jewish life, if *kolel* fellows are viewed as eternal students, doing little of practical value, and living off parental benevolence or public dole.

In response, *kolel* faculty and administration claim that a system of accountability does exist, informal though it may be, and point to the intimate relationship between the student and his instructor, as well as the pressure of peers and colleagues. A student whose performance lags would soon be reprimanded and shamed into improvement. However, personal observation and experience in education raise serious questions regarding the validity of that claim and the simple ability to put such an informal method into effect. In most instances observed in this work, such programs of accountability tend to be highly subjective and haphazard.

The introduction of regular examinations–written, oral, or both–might solve some of the problem. Such an enterprise has been incorporated into the curricula at Yeshiva University, Mechon Hahoyroa, and Kolel Zanz. Detractors claim that it removes the aura of *Torah lishmah*, study for its own sake, especially when performance is linked to stipends and bonuses.

An alternative might be to require regular progress reports in the form of public lectures and written presentations. These could reflect independent research, response to a contemporary problem, review of relevant literature, or novel analyses and insights regarding areas chosen for study that year. Before completion of his program at the *kolel*, and as a prerequisite for graduation, the fellow might be required to submit some piece of original research, much as a graduate student must complete a thesis before the conferral of his degree. The work could be presented to the faculty for their critical appraisal, and the fellow would be called upon to defend his work before a committee of instructors and peers.

This collection of student work should then be included in a journal published by the *yeshivah* or by some other communal institutions. The works might be referred to in more popular publications as well as by *roshei yeshivah* in the course of their own lectures and writing. The image of the nonproductive student might thereby be dispelled. Evidence of student progress–or its absence–could be regularly examined, and the status of the fellow as a member of a genuine academic community would be enhanced. It must be admitted, however, that the author is not optimistic that such changes will occur.

The foregoing has been a broad analysis of the *kolel* and its manifestation as an institution of higher Jewish education in the United States. Much remains yet to be said about its future, its impact upon the quality of Jewish education, and its influence upon Jewish life in general. Important changes are taking place in American Jewish society, and they appear to be restructuring the Jewish community. The extremes are expanding, with increasing numbers of American Jews becoming more strictly observant or more frankly nonobservant. That precarious piece of territory commonly known as the center seems to be thinning rapidly.

FOLLOW-UP SUGGESTIONS

Many issues could not be covered here adequately. Thus, how does the *kolel* confront the reality of Zionism and Jewish nationalism? What is the nature of the society that the *kolel* attempts to create among its fellows and what kinds of children are raised within its bounds? How will the institutions respond to the "crisis of succession" that has already gripped many *kolelim*, caused by the passing of those elderly leaders and founders who served as the last remaining links with their antecedents in prewar Europe?

It is important to look at the material gathered herein with some skepticism. In a community of some 6,000,000 Jews, very few take the small Orthodox group seriously and fewer still are aware of the phenomena that composed the bulk of this project. The *kolel* represents a small and esoteric world closed to the vast majority of American Jews, and skepticism with respect to its influence is, therefore, necessary.

Nevertheless, the *kolel* has displayed surprising growth and vitality in the past generation. Perhaps, within certain confines, it will become the premier institution in Jewish education and a permanent fixture in the Jewish community. Among the wide variety of educational programs available to Jews in America, the *kolel* may yet successfully portray itself as the Ivy League of Jewish scholarship. Given certain internal changes of structure and program, as well as external changes of image and style, there may well be room for optimism.

Appendix 1

Table 4.   The Kolel in America: A Correlation Matrix of Selected Variables

	Length of program	Number of hrs. per day	Age of faculty	Faculty salary	Monthly stipend	No. of children per student	Age of institution	No. of books in library	Student population at founding	Present student population	Mean Student Age
Length of program (in years)	1										
Number of hrs. per day of study	.03	1									
Age of faculty	−.23	−.08	1								
Faculty salary	−.11	.18	−.18	1							
Monthly stipend	.04	.26	−.09	.30	1						
Number of children per student	.53	−.15	−.14	−.06	.14	1					
Age of institution	−.23	.07	.47	.08	−.39	−.52	1				
Number of books in library	−.22	−.11	−.21	.24	.21	−.37	.31	1			
Student population at founding	−.17	−.17	.18	−.39	−.31	.07	.27	−.08	1		
Present student population	−.24	−.05	−.04	−.36	−.37	.07	.50	−.05	.21	1	
Mean student age	−.05	−.44	.18	.32	−.01	.12	−.30	−.41	−.14	.09	1

Table 5. Selected Variables I

Institution	Admission Procedure	Marriage Requirement	Qualification Requirements	Age and Mean	Income, $/ Eligibility Govt. Prog.	Housing	Community Influence
I.							
1. Beth Medrash Govoha	oral interview, references	no	Talmud expertise	21–40 32	160/all govt. programs	no	yes
2. Mir	oral interview, references	yes	Talmud expertise	23–35 29	160–400/yes	no	yes
3. Ner Israel	oral interview, references	yes	Talmud expertise	23–32 28	200–300/yes	some	yes
4. Gur Aryeh	application	yes	Talmud expertise	24–30 28	375–475/yes	no	no
5. Hafez Hayyim	application	no	Talmud expertise	23–30 29	200–640/yes	no	yes
II.							
1. Lubavitch	application	yes	known by administration	23–26 24	220 plus $350 holiday bonus/yes (limited)	no	yes
2. Bobov	application	yes	known by administration	23–35 30	160–400 plus $250 holiday bonus/yes	no	yes
3. Zanz	application	yes	known by administration	19–33 30	250–1500/yes	no	no
4. Gur	application	yes	known by administration	20–30 26	200–1000/yes	no	no

Table 5. *(continued)*

Institution	Admission Procedure	Marriage Requirement	Qualification Requirements	Age and Mean	Income,$/ Eligibility Govt. Prog.	Housing	Community Influence
III.							
1. Yeshiva University	application committee	no	approval *Rosh Kolel* + committee	22–26 24	(1) 1900 annum (2) 4000 annum (3) 10,000/no	dorm no	no
2. Mechon Hahoyroa	seeks candidates + oral exam	yes	expertise in *Horaah*	30–40 35	900–1500/no	no	no
3. Kollel Horabonim	seeks candidates	yes	research knowledge	35–45 40	125 mo./no	no	yes
IV.							
1. Zichron Moshe	oral exam + references	yes	known by administration	24–30 28	320–400/yes (limited)	yes	yes
2. Kolel Bais Avrohom	seeks candidates	yes	learning and service	26–35 30	15,000 annum/no	yes	yes

Table 6. Selected Variables II

Institution	Required Program	Masekhtot, Subjects Studied	Grouping	Lectures/ Curriculum Emphasis	Degrees	Age and Source of Faculty	Faculty Salary
I. 1. Beth Medrash Govoha	1 yr. 6 day/wk 7:40 A.M.– 9:15 P.M.	*B.K., B.M., B.B., Yev., Ked., Git., Ned., musar*	*hevrutah* and *haburah*	weekly/ Talmud	Yor. Yor. Yad. Yad.	40 family and graduates	10,000
2. Mir	3–5 yrs. 6 day/wk 10:00 A.M.– 8:00 P.M.	*B.K., B.M., B.B., San., Ket., Git., Pes., Hullin, musar*	*hevrutah* and *haburah*	weekly/ Talmud	Yor. Yor. Yad. Yad.	60 family and Mir	15,000
3. Ner Israel	3–10 yrs. 5½ day/wk 9:30 A.M.– 6:30 P.M.	*Eruvin, Hullin, Pes., Mikvaot* Codes	*hevrutah*	2 weekly/ Talmud and Codes	Yor. Yor. DTL	40 graduate of school	15,000
4. Gur Aryeh	5 yrs. 5½ day/wk 9:00 A.M.– 6:45 P.M.	*B.K., B.M., B.B., Ned., Git., Kid., Yev., Shab., Ket., Maharal*	*hevrutah,* no *haburah*	2 weekly/ Talmud	optional Yor. Yor. Yad. Yad.	65 yeshivah graduate	15–20,000
5. Hafez Hayyim	3–6 yrs. 6 day/wk 9:35 A.M.– 7:30 P.M.	*B.K., B.M., B.B., Yev., Git., Kid., Ned., Shab., musar*	*hevrutah* and *haburah*	2 weekly/ Talmud	optional Yor. Yor. Yad. Yad.	65 yeshivah graduate	15–20,000

Table 6. *(Continued)*

Institution	Required Program	Masekhtot, Subjects Studied	Grouping	Lectures/ Curriculum Emphasis	Degrees	Age and Source of Faculty	Faculty Salary
II.							
1. Lubavitch	1-3 yrs. 7 day/wk 8:00 A.M.– 7:00 P.M.	*sugyot in Shab., Pes., halakhah, hasidut*	*hevrutah* only	*sugyot* + lectures of Rebbe	no	30s Chabad	10,000
2. Bobov	2 yrs. 7 day/wk 9:30 A.M.– 6:00 P.M.	*sugyot in Moed*	*hevrutah; haburah* once wk	*sugyot*	no	30 family	10,000
3. Zanz	3½–10 yrs. 6 day/wk 5:00 A.M.– 7:00 P.M.	*Shas*	*hevrutah*	Talmud	no	30 family	10,000
4. Gur	2 yrs. 6 day/wk 9:30 A.M.– 6:00 P.M.	*sugyot in Shabbat, Nedarim*	*hevrutah*	*sugyot* and Codes	no	30 family	10,000
III.							
1. Yeshiva University	2 yrs. 5 day/wk 9:00 A.M.– 6:00 P.M.	*Hullin* choice of *R. Hakolel*	*hevrutah and haburah*	Talmud and *halakhah*	Yor. Yor., Yad. Yad	30s yeshivah graduate	15–20,000

2. Mechon Hahoyroa	10–15 yrs. 9:00 A.M.–7:00 P.M.	*Hoshen Mishpat + Even Haezer*	*hevrutah* only	*halakhah*	no	40s family	20,000
3. Kollel Horabonim	2 hrs/day 8:00 P.M.–10:00 P.M.	*halakhic* problems	*hevrutah*	*halakhah*	no	40s founder	?
IV.							
1. Zichron Moshe	3 yrs. 7 day/wk 7:40 A.M.–10:00 P.M.	*yeshivah masekhtot + Hullin*	*hevrutah* occasional *haburah*	Talmud and *horaah*	no	40s founders and yeshivah graduate	15–20,000
2. Kolel Bais Avrohom	2 yrs. 7 day/wk 8:00 A.M.–10:00 P.M.	same as Beth Medrash Govoha	*hevrutah* and *haburah*	Talmud	no	40s founders	15,000

Appendix 2

THE QUESTIONNAIRE

School History and Organization

Date_____

1. Name of School_____
   Address_____
   Telephone_____
   Interviewee_____   Title_____
                                             Position_____
2. Date founded?_____Population at founding?_____
3. Present population?_____No. of buildings?_____
   Description of physical facilities_____
   _____
   _____

4. Reason for founding_____
   _____

5. How do you define Kolel?_____
   _____
   _____

6. School philosophy? What is unique about your Kolel?
   _____
   _____
   _____

7. Qualifications for eligibility: Married_____
   Torah background_____
   Examination_____
   References_____
8. Vertical organization: _____
                           Age level of students_____
9. a. No. of years of required study in your Kolel_____
   b. The stipends For Married?_____
                     For Single?_____ - _____
   c. What scholarships or programs are available for support?_____
       _____
   d. Are there arrangements for parents to help?_____
   e. The typical family?_____
10. No. of classes or groups?_____
    _____
    _____

11. Language of instruction_____

12. Curricular emphasis _____

    _____

    Lithuanian and/or hasidut_____

    _____

    _____

    _____

13. How is the program scheduled: Morning?_____

    Afternoon?_____

    Evening?_____

14. What are the hours a Kolelite must attend?_____

    Days per week?_____

    _____

15. How many tractates are required to be studied?_____

16. Are the students required to get semikhah at the end of their Kolel studies?_____

17. Which tractates are usually covered?_____

    _____

    _____

18. Are there regular shiurim given by rebbeim?_____

19. Is the haburah system practiced?_____ How? _____

    _____

20. What are the qualifications to be a rebbi?

    Please describe_____

21. What are the average salaries?_____

    Are there fringe benefits?_____

    Is there a retirement plan?_____

    Please describe_____

    _____

22. What are the living accommodations offered to your Kolel students?___

    _____

    To the Rebbeim?_____

23. Are your Kolel studies guided towards specific careers?_____

    _____

    What kind?_____

24. Have changes occurred since your Kolel was founded?_____

    _____

    In philosophy_____

    In goals?_____

    In relationship with community in which your Kolel is found?_____

    _____

    In the perspective of outreach to other communities?_____

    _____

    Please explain_____

    _____

25. Is there printed material?_____

    Minutes of meeting?_____

    Brochures?_____

    Yearbook?_____

    Annual journal?_____

    Are official records available?_____

26. Why do yungeleit enter your Kolel?_____

27. What criticism of the Kolel do you feel is unjustified?_____

28. How do you determine which yungeleit should not continue in the Kolel?
_____

29. How are your Kolel graduates or musmakhim placed?_____
_____
_____

AFFILIATION

1. Is your Kolel affiliated with:
   Your Yeshivah?_____
   Torah Umesorah?_____
   Agudath Yisroel?_____
   Local Federation Dept. of Jewish Education?_____
   Other?_____
2. What is the nature of the relationship between the Kolel and
   agency?_____
   Kolel receives funds_____
   Agency supervises_____
   Agency used for consultation_____
   Other_____
   _____

SUPERVISORY

1. Of whom does the supervisory staff consist? Please indicate the part time
   (P) and full time (F) personnel.
   The Rosh Yeshivah_____
   The group Roshei Yeshivah_____
   _____
   The living quarters head(s)_____
2. Who interviews the candidates?_____
   _____
3. In what area of administration does the Rosh Yeshivah spend most of his
   time?   1. Supervision of instruction_____
           2. Supervision of learning_____
           3. Saying shiurim_____
           4. Public relations_____
           5. Conferring with laymen of school_____
           6. Fund raising_____
           7. Other_____
4. a. How is the Rosh Hakolel chosen?_____
      _____
   b. How are the Roshei Yeshivah elected?
      1. Interview_____
      2. References_____
      3. Examination_____
      4. Reputation_____
      5. Previous experience_____
      6. Other_____
5. What factors do you consider most important in engaging a new rabbi or

Rosh Yeshivah?
  1. Scholarship_____
  2. Personality_____
  3. Teaching ability_____
  4. Other_____ Age?_____
6. What is school policy regarding appointments of rebbeim who are relatives of board members?_____
_____

    Relatives of administrative staff?_____
_____

    Relatives of staff members?_____
_____

7. Who are the Masmikhim?_____
8. a. Do you have a Mashgi'ah?_____
   b. By whom was he chosen?_____
   c. On what basis?_____

PERSONAL INTERVIEWS WITH ALUMNI

Kolel name_____
Address_____
  1. In what year did you enter the kolel?_____
  2. What was your background in Torah learning?_____
  3. Why did you join this particular kolel?_____
  4. Were you married?_____Children?_____
  5. What is your wife's attitude towards your learning in the kolel?_____
  6. How many years did you expect to learn in the kolel?_____
  7. In your opinion how does this kolel differ from others?_____
_____
  8. What masekhtos did you learn?_____
_____
  9. Did the kolel fulfill your expectations?_____
10. What would you advise?_____
_____
11. What financial arrangements were made?_____
12. What arrangements for living quarters were provided?_____
_____
13. What was expected of you by the Rosh Yeshivah?_____
_____
14. How many hours a day were you required to study?_____
    Days per week?_____
15. What involvement do you still have with the kolel?_____
_____
16. Would you send your children to a kolel?_____
17. What are you doing now? Profession_____
                            Business_____
                            Rabbinate_____
                            Teaching_____
18. How many hours per week do you now learn?_____
19. Other comments or anecdotes_____
_____
_____

20. Are you a college graduate?_____
21. What is your community involvement?_____
    _____
22. Is there an active alumni organization?_____
    a. **Do they support your Kolel?**_____
    b. Is material produced by Alumni?_____
23. Do you raise funds by a. An Annual Dinner?_____
    b. Journal?_____
    c. Personal gifts?_____
    d. Other sources?_____
24. How many alumni are there?_____

KOLEL STUDENT'S INTERVIEW

KOLEL_____
Name_____
Address_____
Married?_____Children?_____Age?_____
1. a. What prompted you to continue your studies in a Kolel?

    _____
    b. Why did you choose this Kolel?_____
2. What is your Torah background?_____
3. What is the seder of learning?   Per day?_____
   Days per week?_____hofesh?_____
4. What masekhtos are you required to learn?_____
5. What is the method of learning? 1. Shiurim by Rosh Yeshivah_____
   2. Chevrusa_____
   3. Private_____
6. How is the grouping made? 1. By Rosh Yeshivah_____
   2. Voluntarily_____
7. What financial stipend do you earn?_____
8. How is housing arranged?_____
9. What do you intend to do after the Kolel?_____
10. Does the Kolel give semikhah?_____which?_____
11. Are you bound to serve in any communal effort during or after the
    Kolel?_____
12. Do you have any suggestions for younger talmidim about learning
    in a Kolel?_____
    _____
13. How does learning in the Kolel affect your marriage_____
    _____family?_____
14. Would you send your children to learn in a Kolel?_____
15. Is it preferable to learn in a Kolel in your home town or to be
    goleh l'mekom Torah or in Israel?_____
16. a. Are you a college graduate?_____
    b. Will you pursue a post-college or professional degree?_____
       If so, which?_____
17. Do you concentrate on Bekius or Harifus?_____
18. Has the Kolel learning given you a new derekh in learning?_____
    _____

19. Is learning in the Kolel different than learning in a Bais Medrash?
    1. agrees strongly_____
    2. agrees_____
    3. neutral_____
    4. disagrees_____
    5. disagrees strongly_____
20. What rules must you observe to remain in the Kolel?_____
21. Are you familiar with other Kolelim?_____How does this one differ?_____
22. Did your father and/or older brother(s) study in a Kolel?_____
    _____Where?_____
23. **Do you interact with younger talmidim in the Yeshivah?**
    1. a lot_____
    2. somewhat_____
    3. no interaction_____
24. How are you affecting the community in which you are studying?
    e.g. youth programs?_____adult education?_____
    shiurim for women?_____other?_____
25. What is the orientation of this Kolel?_____
    Hasidic?_____
    Litvish?_____
    Other?_____
    What method is emphasized?_____
26. In what language do you study?_____
27. After the regular sedorim, do you engage in any other activities?
    teaching_____
    reach-out_____
    community work_____
    private work_____
    Talmud Torah_____
28. a. Are you influencing hinukh in your community?_____
    how?_____
    b. Are you teaching?_____
29. Is your wife involved in any community activities?_____
    Which?_____
30. Has the Kolel affected Kashruth in the community?
    1. strongly_____
    2. little_____
    3. nothing_____
31. Have you helped the local orthodox rabbi in your community?_____
    _____How?_____
32. How has the presence of the Kolel influenced the stability of the community?_____
33. Do you and your family interact socially with the other avreikhim **and their families?**
    1. often_____
    2. occasionally
    3. never_____
34. Do your children attend the community yeshiva?_____
    If not where do they go?_____
35. Do you have sedorim outside the Kolel?_____
36. How does the stipend you earn help defray your expenses?
    1. all?_____

2. most?_____
3. small part?_____
37. What type of Roshei Yeshivah are there in the Kolel?_____
and how many?_____
38. What do the wives do daily to enable the husband to learn in the Kolel?_____
39. What is your main source of support? Parents?_____
Kolel?_____
Wife?_____
Other?_____

Glossary*

Words set in small caps are defined elsewhere in the glossary.

ADAR. The sixth month of the year corresponding to February or March.

ADMOR. Acronym for *adonaynu*, *moraynu*, *verabaynu*–our lord, our teacher, our master. *Hasidic* title for REBBE.

AGGADAH. All non-*halakhic* interpretations and comments of the Talmudic rabbis.

ASHKENAZI. Coming from an Eastern European background.

AV. The name of the eleventh month corresponding to July or August.

AVREIKH (*avreikhim*, pl.). A young person or fellow.

AYDEM OIF KEST. A son-in-law whose room and board are provided by his father-in-law for a set time.

BAAL HABAYIT (*Ba'alei battim*, pl.). Lay member of a community.

BAAL HABAWS. Yiddish pronunciation of BAAL HABAYIT.

BAAL TESHUVAH (*baale teshuvah*, pl.). Penitent who has returned or joined the Orthodox way of life.

BAIS MEDRASH (ashkenazic pronunciation). A religious study hall.

BAVA BATRA. A Talmudic tractate dealing with the right of possession.

BAVA KAMMA. A Talmudic tractate dealing with civil law concerning compensation for damages and misappropriation of property.

BAVA MEZIAH. A Talmudic tractate dealing with civil law concerning business matters.

BAHURIM. Young single men.

BAHELFER. Tutor, facilitator, or aide; assistant to *melamed*-teacher.

BATLANIM. Time wasters, idlers.

BEKI'UT. Wide-ranging knowledge of the Talmudic text and the standard commentaries.

BERAKHOT. A Talmudic tractate dealing with prayer and blessings.

BET DIN. Court of arbitration, Jewish religious court.

BET MIDRASH. A religious study hall. *See also* BAIS MEDRASH.

BINAH. Literally understanding or discernment. However, it has specialized meaning in Kabbalistic literature.

*Common Hebrew terms included in standard English dictionaries are excluded from this glossary.

BNAI TORAH. Literally, "sons of the Torah," denoting those who make Torah study their life's occupation.

CHABAD. The Lubavitch movement. An acronym for the three terms *hokhmah*, *binah*, and *daat* which represent the basic thought of Lubavitch hasidism.

CHABADNIK. A follower of the Chabad movement.

CHABURA. Also spelled HABURAH, (*haburot*, pl.), cluster, group of *kolel* fellows.

DAAT. Knowledge. It has special meaning in Kabbalistic literature.

DAF YOMI. Literally a daily page. Refers to the system wherein a set page of Talmud is studied every day over a cycle of 7 years.

DAYAN. Judge of a court of Jewish civil law.

DEREKH. A way or system.

DIVREI TORAH. Literally words of Torah, or Torah thoughts.

EKEV. The name of a portion in Deuteronomy.

ELUL. The twelfth month of the year corresponding to August or September.

ELYON. Advanced or superior.

ERETZ. Land of.

ERUVIN. A Talmudic tractate dealing with various domains relating to transferring on Sabbath.

EVEN HA'EZER. One of the four parts of the SHULHAN ARUKH which deals with laws of marriage and divorce.

FARBRENGE (*farbrengen*, pl.). Gathering or assemblage to hear a *hasidic rebbe*'s message.

GADOL (*gedolim*, pl.). An epithet for a giant in Torah knowledge whose leadership is accepted in the Orthodox community.

GET. Jewish bill of divorce.

GITTIN. The name of a Talmudic tractate dealing with laws of divorce.

HABAD. *See* CHABAD.

HABURAH (*haburot*, pl.). *See* CHABURA.

HOKHMAH. Wisdom. It has specialized meaning in Kabbalistic literature.

HALAKHAH. Jewish law.

HEVRUTAH (*hevrutot*, pl.). A pair of students who study together.

HORAAH. *Halakhic* decisions.

KLAUS. Synagogue.

KODASHIM. A section of the six orders of the MISHNAH dealing with the Temple and its sacrifices.

KOSHER. Ritually prepared food in accordance with Jewish law.

KUNTERES. A notebook.

LAMDAN. An acknowledged Talmud scholar.

MAIMONIDES (1135-1204). Rabbi, codifier of law, philosopher.

MASEKHTAH (*masekhtot*, pl.). A Talmudic tractate.

MASHGI'AH (*mashgihim*, pl.) Spiritual overseer and counselor of a YESHIVAH.

MEKHINAH. Preparatory school.

MELAVE MALKAH. Literally, escorting the (Sabbath) queen; name for a festive meal on Saturday night.

MENAHEL. Principal or administrator.

MENAHOT. A Talmudic tractate dealing with flour offerings.

METIVTAH (*mesivtot*, pl. of *metivtah* in the Ashkenazic dialect). Usually refers to a YESHIVAH high school for boys.

MEZUZAH (*mezuzot* pl.). Literally sidepost of a door, a parchment affixed to the doorpost, containing portions from the Torah which mandate placement of the MEZUZAH.

MIDRASH. Rabbinic exposition commentary on the Bible.

MIKVA'OT. A Talmudic tractate dealing with ritual baths.

MIKVEH (*mikva'ot*, pl.). A ritual bathing facility, ritualarium.

MILAH. Ritual circumcision.

MINHA. Afternoon prayer.

MISHMAR. Evening study session usually on Thursday nights.

MISHNAH. The compilation of Talmudic law by R. Judah the Prince (latter half of the second and beginning of the third century C.E.).

MISHNAH BERURAH. A commentary on the *Shulhan Arukh Orah Hayyim* by R. Israel Meir Ha-Kohen of Radun (1838–1933).

MO'ED One of the six divisions of the MISHNAH, dealing with the laws of Sabbath and Jewish holidays.

MOHEL (*mohalim*, pl.). Ritual circumciser.

MUSAR. Instruction aimed at inculcating high levels of ethical and moral conduct.

NASHIM. One of the six divisions of the MISHNAH, dealing with the domestic law.

NEDARIM. A Talmudic tractate dealing with vows and oaths.

NEZKIN. A section of the six orders of the MISHNAH dealing with civil and criminal laws and ethics.

NIDDAH. A Talmudic tractate dealing with laws regarding menstruation.

NISAN. The name of the sixth month of the year, corresponding to April.

OLAM. World or community.

ORAH HAYYIM. Literally way of life. The name of one of the four parts of the *Shulhan Arukh* which deals with daily and regular ritual law.

PERUSHIM. Those who separate themselves from the rest of the community for the sake of Torah study.

PESAHIM. A Talmudic tractate dealing with the laws of Passover.

PEYOT. Traditional *hasidic* sidelocks.

RASHI. The commentator on the written and oral Torah, an acronym for R. Shlomo Izhaki (1040–1105 C.E.), the famous Biblical and Talmudic commentator.

RA'UYI (*re'uyim*, pl.). Worthy or fit.

REBBE (*rebbeim*, pl.) Title of a *hasidic* leader, or a teacher in a YESHIVAH.

REBBETZIN. Wife of a rabbi.

ROSH HAKOLEL. The director of the *kolel*.

ROSH YESHIVAH. The dean and senior professor of the YESHIVAH.

ROSH HABURAH (*roshei haburah*, pl.). A leader of a student cluster seminar.

SAFRUTH. Ritual Hebrew calligraphy.

SANHEDRIN. A Talmudic tractate dealing with courts.

SEDER (*sedarim*, pl.). Order or session.

SEPHARDIC. Related to Spanish or Oriental Jewish practices and pronunciation.

SEMIKHAH. Rabbinic ordination.

SHABBAT. The Talmudic tractate dealing with the laws of the Sabbath.

SHI'UR (*shi'urim*. pl.) A lecture or class in Talmud.

SHLICHUS. Assignment, mission.

SHLITA. An acronym for *sheyihyeh leyamim tovim va' arukim*, literally translated as may he live for good and long years.

SHMUES (*shmuessin*, pl.). Talk, whose theme may be ethical, moral, or pietistic.

SHOHETIM. Ritual slaughterers.

SHNOR. Beg.

SHTENDER. Study lectern.

SHTIBL. *Hasidic* synagogue.

SHULHAN ARUKH. The code of Jewish law compiled by R. Joseph Caro in Safed (1488–1575).

SHULHAN ARUKH HARAV. The Code of Jewish Law composed by R. Shneur Zalman of Lyady (1745–1813).

SOFER (*soforim*, pl.). Ritual scribe.

SUGYA (*sugyot*, pl.). A Talmudic subject.

SUKKAH. A Talmudic tractate dealing with the laws of the festival of Tabernacles.

TALESIM. Prayer shawls.

TALMID HAKHAM. Rabbinic scholar.

TALMUD TORAH. The study of Torah, also refers to an afternoon Hebrew school.

TALMUDIC. Pertaining to the Talmud.

TEFILLIN (also spelled *tephillin*). Ritual phylacteries.

TIFERES. Splendor.

TISHA B'AV. The ninth day of Av, observed as a fast day commemorating the destruction of the first and second temples of Jerusalem.

T.J., TALMUD JERUSHALMI. The Palestinian version of the Talmud.

TORAH. The Pentateuch, also the entire body of Jewish law.

TORAH LISHMAH. The study of Torah for its own sake, i.e., pure study without a utilitarian goal.

TORAH UMESORAH. A national organization for traditional Jewish schools in America.

TUR. The compilation of Jewish law by R. Yaakov B. Asher (1270?–1340).

VA'AD (*va'adim*, pl.). Group that meets regularly to study MUSAR.

VA'AD HAKELAL. General committee.

VA'AD HAHAZZALAH. Committee for the rescue of Jews during World War II.

YAD. The alternate name of Maimonides' code, *Mishneh Torah*.

YADIN YADIN. Rabbinic ordination degree conferred for expertise in Jewish civil law.

YARHEI KALLAH. Literally months of assembly. Today, it refers to a specific time of Torah study by laymen and rabbis.

YESHIVOT GEDOLOT. Secondary and higher level *yeshivot*.

YESHIVOT KETANOT. Elementary level schools.

YEVAMOT. The Talmudic tractate dealing with levirate marriage.

YISHUV. The Jewish settlement in Palestine prior to the emergence of the Jewish State of Israel.

YOMA. A Talmudic tractate dealing with the laws of Yom Kippur.

YOREH DE'AH (pronounced *yohreh day'ah*). One of the four parts of the *Shulhan Arukh* which deals with ritual law.

YOREH YOREH. The ordination degree conferred for expertise in ritual law.

YUNGERMAN (*yungeleit*, pl.). Literally a young man, a *kolel* fellow.

ZIZIT. Ritual fringes worn on the corners of a four-cornered garment.

Notes

INTRODUCTION

1. The literature regarding American Jewish education is considerable. Among the major studies are William B. Helmreich, *The World of the Yeshiva: An Intimate Portrait of Orthodox Jewry* (New York: Free Press, 1982); Gilbert Klaperman, *The Story of Yeshiva University* (New York: Macmillan, 1969); Isidor Margolis, *Jewish Teacher Training Schools in the U.S.* (New York: Mizrachi-Hapoel Hamizrachi, 1964); Alexander Dushkin, *Jewish Education in New York City* (New York: Board of Jewish Education, 1913); and Alvin I. Schiff, *The Jewish Day School in America* (New York: Jewish Education Committee Press, 1966).

2. The estimate emerged from an interview with Dov Lesser of Torah Umesorah, the National Association of Jewish Day Schools, in December 1981. R. Lesser is Director of Placement in Torah Umesorah.

3. A good description of the method of study common in Lithuanian-style *kolelim* can be found in Harry Austryn Wolfson, *Crescas' Critique of Aristotle* (Cambridge: Harvard University Press, 1929), pp. 24–27. See Gedaliah Alon, "Yeshivot Lita," in *Mehkarim B'toldot Yisrael*, Vol. II (Jerusalem, 1957), pp. 1–11.

4. The structure of study in the traditional *hasidic* community is described by Hillel Seidman, "Yeshivat Ez Hayyim D'Klezk," in S.K. Mirsky, ed., *Mosdot Torah B'Ayropah Bevinyanam Uv'Hurbanam* (New York: Histadruth Ha'Ivrit B'America, 1956), pp. 239–42.

5. R. Dov Lesser, interview with author, Brooklyn, N.Y., December 1981.

6. It should be noted that transliterations of foreign terms are in accordance with the notation system described in the *Encyclopedia Judaica* (Jerusalem: Keter, 1972), Vol. 1, pp. 90–91. However, in coveying direct quotes or proper names, the author has respectfully retained the spelling used by the source.

7. The Association of Advanced Rabbinical and Talmudic Schools is a national, voluntary association founded by eight of the major Rabbinical and Talmudic schools in 1944. It was originally established as the "Council of Roshei Yeshivos." It was organized in 1971 and an independent commission was invited to study the programs in the affiliate institutions and to formulate recommendations. As a result of the recommendations, AARTS established an Accreditation Commission. An accredited *yeshivah* is eligible for various types of government aid, such as work-study and Basic Education Opportunity Grants (BEOG). One of the requirements in the application for the school's accreditation is the self-study, which is basically a comparison of the school to the standards established by AARTS. The office of AARTS is located at 175 Fifth Avenue, New York City. A *Handbook of the Accreditation Commission* is available, listing the 27 accredited institutions and 19 institutions granted candidate status as of June 1982. Almost all of these institutions claim to have a "graduate division," i.e., a *kolel*.

8. Periodical indexes and reference sources considered include University Microfilms International, *The Education Index, Social Sciences Index* (New York: Wilson, 1970–1982); *Index to Jewish Periodicals* (Cleveland: College of Jewish Studies, 1970–82); and *Periodicals in Jewish Education* (New York: Council of Jewish Education, 1982).

9. Nisson Wolpin, "The Community Kolel: Reaching Out With Torah," *The Jewish Observer* (October 1979), pp. 19–26; and Mendel Rokeach, "The Kolel: American Phase," *Jewish Life* (May–June 1963), pp. 13–21.

10. Schiff, *The Jewish Day School in America*, p. 238.

11. Helmreich, *The World of the Yeshiva*, pp. 257–65.

12. David Singer, "The Yeshivah World," *Commentary* (October 1976), pp. 70–73.

13. Sidney R. Lewitter, "A School for Scholars: The Beth Medrash Govoha, The Rabbi Aaron Kotler Jewish Institute of Higher Learning in Lakewood, New Jersey" (Ed. D. diss., Rutgers University, 1981).

14. Samuel K. Mirsky, ed., *Mosdot Torah B'Ayropah Bevinyanam Uv'hurbanam* (New York: Histadruth Ha'Ivrit B'America, 1956).

PART ONE: THE KOLEL IN AMERICA

1. The point is delineated on a number of occasions. See, for example, Shabbat 127a, "the study of Torah is equal to all." See also Kiddushin 40b and Sanhedrin 7a.

2. Menahot 110a.

3. Samuel K. Mirsky, ed., Introduction to *Mosdot Torah B'Ayropah Bevinyanam Uv'hurbanam*. See also Kiddushin 49b.

4. Kiddushin 29b.

5. Maimonides, *Hilkhot Talmud Torah, Yad,* 1:8. Author's translation.

6. Ibid., 3:10. Author's translation.

7. See Mirsky, *Mosdot Torah*, pp. 2–6.

8. For a description of the *halukkah* system, see B.Z. Gat, *Ha-Yishuv ha-Yehudi B'Eretz Yisrael* (Jerusalem, 5723), Chap. 4, and M. Solomon. *Three Generations in the Yishuv* (Hebrew) (Jerusalem, 5702), pp. 23ff. The word *kolel* is a derivative of the Hebrew verb *kll* and is related to the word *klal*, which means community or group.

9. For information about R. Israel Salant and the *musar* movement, see Dov Katz, *The Musar Movement, Its History, Leading Personalities and Doctrines*, trans. Leonard Oschry (Tel Aviv: Orly Press, 1977), Vols. 1 and 2; Kopul Rosen, *Rabbi Israel Salanter and the Musar Movement* (London, 1943); Joseph Elias, "Israel Salanter," in Leo Jung, ed., *Jewish Leaders 1750–1940* (Jerusalem: Boys Town Jerusalem Press, 1964), pp. 199–211; Menahem G. Glenn, *Israel Salanter, Religious-Ethical Thinker: The Story of a Religious-Ethical Current in 19th Century Judaism*, published for the Dropsie College for Hebrew and Cognate Learning (New York: Bloch, 1953); and Lester Eckman, *The History of the Musar Movement 1840–1945* (New York: Shengold Publishers, 1975).

10. For a full analysis of R. Kotler's efforts in the establishment of Beth Medrash Govoha, see Mendel Rokeach, "The Kollel: American Phase," *Jewish Life* (May–June 1963), pp. 13–21.

11. Beth Medrash Elyon ceased to operate as an active *kolel* in the late 1970s. For a description of R. Mendlowitz's career in Jewish education and communal affairs, see Alexander Gross and Joseph Kaminetsky, "Shraga Feivel Mendlowitz," in Leo Jung, ed., *Men of the Spirit* (New York: Bloch, 1964), pp. 533–61. See also Hillel Seidman, *Shraga Feivel Mendlowitz* (Hebrew) (New York: Shengold Publishers, 1976).

12. R. Jacob Ruderman, interview with author, Baltimore, Md., April 1982.

PART TWO: THE KOLELIM

1. See *Bulletin—Undergraduate Division*, Beth Medrash Govoha (Lakewood, Beth Medrash Govoha, 1977), hereafter referred to as *Bulletin*.

2. See Hillel Seidman, "Yeshivat Ez Hayyim D'Kletsk," in S.K. Mirsky, ed., *Mosdot Torah*, pp. 229-38.

3. Moses and Hayyim Feifer, alumni who found refuge in Shanghai during World War II, interviews with author, February 1982. See also David Kranzler, *Japanese, Nazis and*

Jews: The Jewish Refugee Community of Shanghai, 1938-1945 (New York: Yeshiva University, 1976); and Zorach Warhaftig, *Palit v'Sarid* (Jerusalem, 1984).

4. *Bulletin*, pp. 11–14.

5. R. Eliezer Kuperman, Director of Student Relations at Beth Medrash Govoha, interview with author, Lakewood, N.J., January 1982.

6. *Bulletin*, pp. 41–42.

7. R. Pesach Levovitz, congregational spiritual leader, Lakewood, N.J., telephone conversation with author, June 1982.

8. Kuperman interview, January 1982. See also *Bulletin*, pp. 33–36, 54.

9. R. Shneur Kotler, late *Rosh Yeshivah* of Beth Medrash Govoha, interview with author, Lakewood, N.J., January 1982. R. Kotler stressed the importance of the *haburah* as a training ground for future rabbis and teachers and as a laboratory for teaching the social value of friendship.

10. Kuperman interview, January 1982; Noach Klor, a *kolel* student, and R. Shmuel Mayer, an alumnus. interviews with author, Lakewood, N.J., January 1982.

11. *Bulletin*, pp. 57–58. Among those who have examined these *kolel* students are such authorities as R. Moshe Feinstein, R. Moshe Bick, and R. Shimon Eider.

12. Kuperman interview, January 1982.

13. Interview with *kolel* fellow, January 1982.

14. Interview with *kolel* wives, January 1982.

15. Details of these programs are gleaned from the *Bulletin*, pp. 37–41.

16. Ibid., pp. 48–49.

17. Kuperman interview, January 1982.

18. Interview with *kolel* fellows, February 1982.

19. See *Alumni Newsletter*, a bimonthly offset publication first issued in March 1981, containing *"Shiurim shmuesen Aggadah and Divrei Torah,"* as well as "News of the Yeshiva, its Talmidim, Faculty and Alumni."

20. Sidney R. Lewitter, "A School for Scholars: The Beth Medrash Govoha, The Rabbi Aaron Kotler Jewish Institute of Higher Learning in Lakewood, New Jersey," (Ed.D. diss., Rutgers University, 1981,) pp. 33–34.

21. David Singer, "The Yeshivah World," *Commentary* (October 1976), p. 72.

22. Kuperman interview, January 1982.

23. Joseph D. Epstein, "Mir," in S.K. Mirsky, ed., *Mosdot Torah*, pp. 87–132.

24. Shrage Moshe Kalmanowitz, *Rosh Yeshivah* of Mirrer Yeshivah Central Institute, interviews with author, Brooklyn N.Y., September–October 1981. See also Rabbi Nahum Yacow, *The History of the Mir Yeshiva in America* (New York: Mir Yeshiva Central Institute, 1978).

25. *Mir Yeshiva Central Institute: Self-Study* (New York: Association of Advanced Rabbinical and Talmudic Schools, 1975), pp. 9–20. Rabbi Moses Handelsman, Executive Director of the Mir Yeshiva, interview with author, Brooklyn N.Y., October 1981.

26. Handelsman interview, September 1981.

27. Kalmanowitz interview, October 1981.

28. David Lieff, former President of the Rabbinical Board of Flatbush, interview with author, Brooklyn, N.Y., November 1981.

29. Information regarding the *haburot* was provided in March 1982 in an interview with R. Eliezer Ginzburg, a faculty member in charge of *haburah* assignments.

30. Faculty member of the Mirrer Yeshiva, interview with author, January 1982. The source is unidentified, at the interviewee's request.

31. Handelsman interview, October 1981.

32. Moshe Schoenblum, a student at the Mir *kolel*, interview with author, Brooklyn, N.Y., January 1982.

33. Based on data provided by the Beth Din of the Rabbinical Council of America and by the Rabbinical Alliance of America, February 1982.

34. Kalmanowitz interview, September 1981.

35. Nahum Yacow, *The History of the Mir Yeshiva in America.*

36. Epstein, "Mir," in *Mosdot Torah*, pp. 87–132.

37. Alvin I. Schiff, *The Jewish Day School in America*, p. 146.

38. This brief review of the history of Yeshiva Ner Israel is based upon Yaakov Kaminetsky, "Filling the Void: Reflections on the Passing of a Godol," *Jewish Observer* (October 1976), pp. 15–19; Issac Ever, *Harav Yehuda Heschel Levenberg: Zein Leben und Kampf* (Cleveland: Ivry, 1939); and William Helmreich, *The World of the Yeshiva: An Intimate Portrait of Orthodox Jewry* (New York: Free Press, 1983).

39. See the *Ner Israel Rabbinical College Bulletin* (Baltimore: Ner Israel, 1982), p. 8, hereafter referred to as *Bulletin.*

40. Rabbi Jacob Ruderman, *Rosh Yeshivah* at Ner Israel, and Samuel Glazer, Executive Director of the Ner Israel Kolel, interviews with author, Baltimore, Md., May 1982.

41. Ruderman and Glazer interviews, May 1982.

42. Ruderman interview, May 1982; see also *Yeshiva Ner Israel: Self-Study* (New York: Association of Advanced Rabbinical and Talmudic Schools, 1981), hereafter referred to as *Self-Study.*

43. Students of the Ner Israel Kolel, interview with author, May 1982.

44. *Bulletin*, p. 26.

45. *NI Self-Study*, p. 14.

46. *Bulletin*, pp. 26–27.

47. Glazer interview, May 1982.

48. Iranian *kolel* students at Ner Israel, interviews with author, May 1982.

49. *Kuntres Or HaKolel* (Baltimore: Ner Israel, 1980). Twenty have been published to date.

50. This material is based on interviews with ten Ner Israel Kolel families, conducted in May 1982.

51. Interview with a student of the Ner Israel Kolel, May 1982, who has requested to remain unidentified.

52. *NI Self-Study*, p. 3.

53. Alvin I. Schiff, *The Jewish Day School in America,* pp. 45–46.

54. Sidney Lieberman, "A Historical Study of the Development of the Yeshiva High School Curriculum," (Ph.D. diss., Yeshiva University, 1959), p. 79.

55. William B. Helmreich, *The World of the Yeshiva,* p. 35.

56. See, for example, the brochure *Purpose* (New York: Yeshiva Chaim Berlin, n.d.), p. 2.

57. For a laudatory review of the early years of the Kolel Gur Aryeh, see the various essays in *Tenth Anniversary Souvenir Journal* (New York: Yeshiva Chaim Berlin, 1966), published by the Gur Aryeh Institute office.

58. Shmuel Wolman, director of the Kolel Gur Aryeh, interview with author, Brooklyn, N.Y., April 1982.

59. *Yeshiva Chaim Berlin: Self-Study* (New York: Association of Advanced Rabbinical and Talmudic Schools, 1975), p. 1-1, hereafter referred to as *YCB Self-Study.*

60. Interview with fellows of the Kolel Gur Aryeh, April 1982.

61. In an exception to this statement, *kolel* students did participate in a rally to protest a pornographic shop that was opened in the area in January 1982.

62. The Talmudic cycle at Yeshiva Chaim Berlin is Kiddushin, Gittin, Ketubot, Bava Kama, Bava Meziah, Bava Batra, Shabbat, Yevamot, and Nedarim.

63. Wolman interview, April 1982; Dov Fink, telephone conversation with author,

questionnaire, 18 April 1982.

64. Wolman and Fink interviews, April 1982.

65. *YCB Self-Study*, pp. 1–3.

66. Interview with *kolel* fellows, April 1982.

67. See, for example, Nechama Bakst, "Woman at the Crossroads," *The Jewish Observer* (February 1982), pp. 14–16.

68. R. Aharon Schechter, *Rosh Yeshivah* at Chaim Berlin, interview with author, Brooklyn, N.Y., April 1982.

69. Wolman interview, April 1982.

70. Schechter interview, April 1982.

71. Israel Meir Hakohen, *Mishnah Berurah* (Jerusalem: Monzon, 1946); Israel Meir Hakohen, *Sefer Shmirat Halashon* (Jerusalem: Vaad Sh'mirat Halashon, 1967). See also Moses M. Yosher, "Israel Meir Ha-Kohen, the Hafetz Hayyim," in Leo Jung, ed., *Jewish Leaders* (Jerusalem: Boys Town Jerusalem Press, 1974), pp. 457–73.

72. *Yeshivat Rabbi Israel Meir Ha-Kohen: Self-Study* (New York: Association of Advanced Rabbinical and Talmudic Schools, 1975), p. 3, hereafter referred to as *Ha-Kohen Self-Study*.

73. On the founding of the *yeshivah*, see Eli B. Greenwald, "The Education of American Rabbis, 1867–1939," (Ph.D. diss., Dropsie University, 1979), Chap. 5. On the conflict between Leibowitz and Mendlowitz, see William Helmreich, *The World of the Yeshiva*, pp. 26–29.

74. *Yeshivat Rabbi Israel Meir Ha-Kohen: Self-Study Update* (New York: Association of Advanced Rabbinical and Talmudical Schools, 1981), p. 4, hereafter referred to as *Self-Study Update*.

75. Henoch Leibowitz, *Rosh Yeshivah* of Kolel Ner David, telephone conversation with author, March 1982.

76. *Self-Study Update*, p. 16.

77. R. Daniel Tropper, *mashgi'ah* of Kolel Ner David, telephone conversation with author, questionnaire, November 1981.

78. R. Jeffrey Adlerstein, an alumnus of Kolel Ner David residing in Los Angeles, questionnaire, 27 January 1982.

79. R. Mayer May, alumnus of Kolel Ner David, interview with author, January 1982.

80. Tropper interview, November 1981.

81. *Ha-Kohen Self-Study*, p. 24.

82. Interview with eight *kolel* students who have served in the program, January 1982.

83. These are Bava Kamma, Bava Meziah, Bava Batra, Yevamot, Gittin, Kiddushin, Nedarim, and Shabbat.

84. Aside from the seven-year cycle, students of the *kolel* may cover Hullin, Pesahim, and Niddah, among other tractates.

85. *Yeshivah* literature, published in a calendar for the year 1981–82.

86. The comment was made in an interview with a member of the Talmud faculty of Yeshiva University who preferred anonymity, in March 1982.

87. The author was a member of the committee that helped establish this arrangement with Queens College in December 1971.

88. Interview with *kolel* students, January 1982.

89. Leibowitz interview, November 1981.

90. Interview with *kolel* wives, March 1982.

91. Interview with alumni, April 1982.

92. Interviews with students and alumni, March 1982.

93. The author had the opportunity to visit these summer retreats in July 1970.

94. Interview with alumni and their wives, March 1982.

95. Helmreich, *The World of the Yeshiva*, p. 71.

96. Ibid., p. 362 n. 6.

97. For a review of the life of Rabbi Schneur Zalman of Liadi, see Charles B. Chavel, "Shneyur Zalman of Liady," in Leo Jung, ed., *Jewish Leaders*, pp. 53–76.

98. See *The Lubavitcher Rebbe* (New York: Merkos L'inyonei Chinuch, 1978).

99. Hillel Seidman, "Yeshiva Lubavitch," in Samuel Mirsky, ed., *Mosdot Torah*, p. 337.

100. Abraham H. Glitzenstein, *Tomchei T'mimim* (New York: United Yeshivot Tomchei T'mimim Lubavitch, 1969).

101. Seidman, "Yeshiva Lubavich," *op. cit.*, pp. 338–40.

102. *Central Yeshiva Tomchei T'mimim: Self-Study* (New York: Association of Advanced Rabbinical and Talmudic Schools, 1976), p. 4, hereafter referred to as *CY Self-Study*. See also *The Lubavitcher Rebbe*, p. 7.

103. Rabbi Joseph I. Heller, *Rosh Hakolel* of Chabad-Lubavitch, interview with author, Brooklyn, N.Y., January 1982.

104. *Central Yeshiva Tomchei T'mimim-Lubavitch, Catalogue 1979–1980* (New York: Chabad-Lubavitch, 1980), pp. 25–26, hereafter referred to as *Catalogue*.

105. R. Moshe Kotlarsky, director of development of Chabad Houses, interview with author, Brooklyn, N.Y., December 1981.

106. Heller interview, January 1982; and Mendel Rosenfeld, *kolel* student, interview with author, January 1982.

107. Interview with *kolel* students, January 1982.

108. *CY Self-Study*, pp. 44–45.

109. Ibid., pp. 18, 26.

110. Ibid., p. 26. Also, R.M.A. Hodakov, treasurer of Machne Israel, the Chabad Social Welfare Organization, interview with author, Brooklyn, N.Y., March 1982.

111. Interview with several *kolel* wives, January 1982.

112. *Catalogue*, pp. 43–44.

113. Interview with *kolel* wives, January 1982.

114. Ibid.

115. *Catalogue*, p. 40.

116. Heller interview, January 1982.

117. The early development of the Bobover community is reviewed in Zvi Halevi Ish Horowitz, *Letoldot Hakehilot B'Polin* (Jerusalem: Mossad Harav Kook, 1978), pp. 478–80; and Louis Jacobs, *Hasidic Thought* (New York: Behrman House, 1976), pp. 210–15.

118. *Yeshiva Eitz Chaim of Bobov: Self-Study* (New York: AARTS, 1975), p. 7, hereafter referred to as *YEC Self-Study*.

119. R.Yonasan Goldberger, *Rosh Hakolel* of Kolel Avreichim of Bobov, interview with author, Brooklyn, N.Y., May 1982.

120. *YEC Self-Study*, p. 38.

121. Interview with *kolel* fellows, May 1982.

122. R. Morris Schmidman, executive director of the Boro Park Council of Jewish Organizations, telephone conversation with author, June 1982.

123. The opinion of *kolel* fellows in an interview held in May 1982.

124. *YEC Self-Study*, p. 69.

125. Ibid., p. 20.

126. Ibid., p. 26.

127. *Kolel* fellows interview, May 1982.

128. Goldberger interview, May 1982.

129. *YEC Self-Study*, pp. 95–98.

130. Ibid., pp. 78-95

131. Goldberger and *kolel* fellows interview, May 1982.

132. See Section 7 for a fuller description of the Halberstam family and its rabbinic branches.

133. R. Jekuthiel Judah Halberstam, *Minhat Yehudah V'Yerushalayim* (Union City, N.J.: Yisroel Sovo Institute, 1979), p. 215.

134. R. Jekuthiel Judah Halberstam, Klausenberge *Rebbe*, interview with author, Union City, N.J., 8 June 1982.

135. In addition, Azriel Tauber, a wealthy financier from Monsey, New York, has agreed to provide an additional $150 per month for students who will sit for examinations on twenty folio of Talmud each month. For an analysis of Tauber's Mechon Hahoyroa, see Section 11.

136. Interestingly, the son of a local reform rabbi has become a Zanz *hasid* and is a student at its *yeshivah*. Interview, June 1982.

137. Yankel Mashinsky, a senior *kolel* fellow, interview with author, Union City, N.J., June 1982.

138. Mashinsky interview, June 1982.

139. Interview with the *rosh hakolel*, June 1982.

140. R. Jekuthiel Judah Halberstam, *Shefa Hayyim* (Union City, N.J.: Yisroel Sovo, 1980); and *Minhat Yehuda V'Yerushalayim*.

141. Joseph Deitch, *Seder HaShehitah V'Hakhsharat HaBasar HaNehugim B'Kehillataynu K.K. Zanz Klauzenberg* (Union City, N.J.: Zanz Klausenberg, 1979).

142. Mashinsky interview, June 1982.

143. Mashinsky interview, June 1982.

144. Halberstam, *Shefa Hayyim*, pp. 128–29.

145. See, for example, B. Jacobson, "Torah Returns to Its Lodging," *Zanz* (14 May 1982), p. 3.

146. Halberstam, *Shefa Hayyim*, p. 127.

147. R. Eliyahu Fisher, *rosh hakolel* of Gur, interview with author, Brooklyn, N.Y., June 1982.

148. Ibid.

149. Interview with *kolel* fellows, June 1982.

150. Fisher interview, June 1982.

151. Fisher interview, May 1982.

152. Ibid.

153. This history can be reviewed in Gilbert Klaperman, *The Story of Yeshiva University* (New York: Macmillan, 1960); Aaron Rothkoff, *Bernard Revel: Builder of American Jewish Orthodoxy* (Philadelphia: Jewish Publication Society, 1972); I. Margolis, *Jewish Teacher Training Schools in the United States* (New York: Mizrahi Hapoel-Hamizrahi, 1964); Eli B. Greenwald, *Rabbinic Education in the United States*, (Ph.D. diss., Dropsie University, 1975); and Louis Bernstein, *Challenge and Mission: The Emergence of the English Speaking Orthodox Rabbinate* (New York: Shengold, Publishers, 1982).

154. Dr. Bernard Revel, acclaimed as a rabbinic prodigy at the age of 6, arrived in the United States at the age of 21, studied at RIETS, and then completed graduate degrees at New York University and Dropsie College, receiving that institution's first doctoral degree. His publications and research reflect precisely the kind of synthesis of Torah and secular studies that have become the hallmark of Yeshiva University. See Rothkoff, *Bernard Revel*.

155. A discussion of Rabbi Israel Meir HaKohen and the American institution that bears his name can be found in Section 5.

156. Charles Bendheim, member of the RIETS Board of Directors, telephone conversation with author, March 1982; Seymour Cyperstein, son of the first *rosh hakolel*, telephone conversation with author, March 1982. It is revealing that in Klaperman's entire study of the institution's history, there is no reference to the *kolel*. See Klaperman, *The Story of Yeshiva University*.

157. R. Israel Miller, Vice President of Yeshiva University, telephone conversation with author, June 1982.

158. It should be noted that a fourth program has been established bearing the title Chaver Kolel Program. This unit is a one-year curriculum of study for those who have no intention of pursuing Jewish scholarship or entering communal service, but who would like to intensify their level of understanding. While it serves a most laudable objective, it has not been included here because it is not a *kolel* by conventional definition. Its students receive no stipends, nor does it fit any of the typologies established here. Indeed, the use of the term "*kolel*" may well be a misnomer. Essentially, the Chaver Kolel Program is a formal study program for those who will enter other professions.

159. R. Norman Lamm, President of Yeshiva University, interviews with author, New York, N.Y., March 1982, and several *kolel* fellows, March 1982.

160. *Kolel* fellows interview, March 1982. R. Herschel Schachter, *rosh hakolel* at Marcos and Adina Katz Kolel, interview with author, May 1982.

161. R. Aharon Kahn, *rosh hakolel* of Kolel Elyon, interview with author, New York, N.Y., March 1983.

162. Since the initial investigation, some of this confusion has been eliminated and the *kolel* has moved in the direction of community service.

163. Interview with *kolel* fellows, February 1982.

164. Interview with *kolel* wives, March 1982.

165. Interview with *kolel* fellow of the Marcos and Adina Katz Kolel, April 1982.

166. Kahn interview, March 1983.

167. R. Azriel Tauber, *rosh hakolel* at Machon Hahoyroa, interview with author, Monsey, N.Y., June 1982.

168. The source for this classical partnership is Genesis Rabbah 98:12. For an *halakhic* treatment of this subject, see R. Moshe Feinstein, "The Partnership of Yissachar and Zebulun." *Am Hatorah,* 5, (1982), pp. 5-31.

169. Leviticus Rabbah 2:1; Ecclesiastes Rabbah 7:28.

170. See, for example, *Der Yid.* 13 November 1981; *Algemeiner Journal,* 26 March 1982; *Ha' audah* 28 Iyar 1982; *Hamodiah* 21 May 1982; and Aryek Kaplan, "Variations on the Yissachar-Zevelun Theme," *The Jewish Observer* (January 1978), pp. 23–26.

171. Tauber interview, June 1982.

172. See Y. Menahem, "Der Bais Din Fun Kolel Mechon L'horaya in Monsey," *Dos Yiddishe Vort* (Iyar-Sivan 1983), p. 42.

173. Tauber interview, June 1982.

174. Interview with *kolel* students and their wives, June 1982.

175. R. Yakov T. Weiner, director of the *mekhinah* program, interview with author, Monsey, N.Y., June 1982.

176. Tauber interview, June 1982.

177. The Veshinantem Program and its success were described in an interview with R. Yakov Kaminetsky, former Dean of Yeshiva Torah Vodaath, in January 1983. The

venerable sage now resides in Monsey and has been intimately involved in the development of the curriculum and structure of the Tauber Kolel. The name Veshinantam literally means "and thou shalt teach them diligently." See Deuteronomy 6:7.

178. Azriel Tauber, ed., *Yisaschar B' ohalekhah* (Monsey, N.Y.: Mechon Hahoyroa, 1979).

179. R. Leib Landesman, Dean of Kollel Horabonim, interviews with author, Monsey and Queens, N.Y., June 1982.

180. Landesman interview, June 1982.

181. Interview with *kolel* fellows, June 1982. See also Aryeh Kaplan, "A Get in Monsey," *The Jewish Observer* (December 1976), pp. 15–19.

182. *Kolel* fellows interview, June 1982.

183. Ibid.

184. Landesman interview and *kolel* fellows, June 1982.

185. Interview with *kolel* fellow, June 1982.

186. Interview with an alumnus, June 1982.

187. See Yaacov Spivak, "The Kollel Horabonim: Torah Answers to Explosive Questions," *The World Jewish Tribune*, 18 January 1980; Yaacov Spivak, "The Jewish Divorce and Those Who 'Forget' to Get a Get," *The World Jewish Tribune*, 7 March 1980, pp. 11–12; and Kaplan, "A Get in Monsey."

188. The opinion was expressed by a local rabbi in Monsey, New York, in an interview in June 1982. The opinion was confirmed by several other local rabbis and students at other *kolelim*.

189. The Kollel Bais Avrohom has particular significance within the context of this study. It was the writer's original intention to include the community *kolelim* of Chicago, Detroit, Pittsburgh, and Denver as part of this study. However, after serious discussion with Dov Lesser of Torah Umesorah, it was found that Kollel Bais Avrohom has served as the model for other community *kolelim*. The analysis of all four community *kolelim* was therefore deemed unnecessary.

190. R. Fasman, founder and dean of Kollel Bais Avrohom, Los Angeles, Ca., interview with author, January 1982.

191. Fasman interview, January 1982. It should be noted that a similar institution was successfully established in Toronto prior to the founding of Kollel Bais Avrohom of Los Angeles. See Nisson Wolpin, "The Community Kolel: Reaching Out With Torah," *The Jewish Observer* (October 1979), pp. 19-26. For a brief discussion of a similar experiment in Australia, see Nisson Wolpin, "Higher Horizons Down Under: An Australian Torah Connection," *The Jewish Observer* (November 1981), p. 26.

192. "Excerpts from Recent Remarks of R. Chaim Fasman Regarding Aims, Activities and Achievement," Kollel Bais Avrohom of Los Angeles. Mimeographed (n.d.).

193. The point is emphasized in the *Kollel Bais Avrohom Newsletter*, September–October 1981, and November–December 1981.

194. Interview with *kolel* families, January 1982.

195. Interview with *kolel* fellows, January 1982.

196. "Excerpts from Recent Remarks," *op. cit.*

197. Fasman interview, January 1982.

198. R. Abba Gorelick, dean, and Robert Gibber, executive director of the *yeshivah*, interviews with author, Fallsburg, N.Y., July and August 1983.

199. From a letter from interested laymen to the directors of the *yeshivah*, August 1975.

200. *Kolel* fellows Bezalel Weiderman and Chaim Borny, interviews with author, Fallsburg, N.Y., 17 August 1983.

201. The comment was made by a member of the local police department who preferred anonymity, in an interview held in August 1983.

202. Interestingly, the *kolel* fellows indicated that no formal stipulation about residency exists, whereas the administration officially requires a minimum three-year residency. Despite this specified time factor, the fellows feel that the *kolel* is their home for as long as they wish to continue to study.

203. This method encourages the practical utilization of the talents of the *kolel* fellows. *Kolel* fellows' interview, August 1983.

204. Gorelick interview, July 1983.

205. Gorelick and *kolel* fellows' interview, August 1983.

206. Gorelick and *kolel* fellows' interview, August 1983.

207. Gibber interview, August 1983.

208. Gorelick interview, July 1983.

209. The fellows told of one student who was encouraged to leave by innuendo.

PART THREE: ANALYSIS OF DATA

1. For an overview of the use of correlations in similar research, see Paul G. Hoel, *Introduction to Mathematical Statistics* (New York: John Wiley and Sons, 1966), pp. 160-63; and Hubert Blalock, *Social Statistics* (New York: McGraw-Hill, 1979), Chapters 17 and 18. The interpretation of the figures in the correlation matrix is drawn from Paul G. Hoel, *Introduction to Mathematical Statistics*.

2. Blalock, p. 18. Technically, these variables are called "interval" or "ratio level."

3. Ibid., Chap. 15.

Bibliography

Books

Alon, Gedaliah. "Yeshivot Lita." In Vol. 2 of *Mehkarim B'toldot Yisrael*. Jerusalem, 1957.

Blalock, Hubert. *Social Statistics*. New York: McGraw-Hill, 1979.

Chavel, Charles B. "Shneyur Zalman of Liady." In *Jewish Leaders 1750–1940*, edited by Leo Jung, 51–76. Jerusalem: Boys Town Jerusalem Publishers, 1964.

Deitch, Joseph. *Seder HaShehitah V'Hakhsharat HaBasar HaNehugim B'kehylataynu K.K. Zanz Klausenberg*. Union City, N.J.: Zanz Klausenberg, 1979.

Dushkin, Alexander. *Jewish Education in New York City*. New York: Bureau of Jewish Education, 1918.

Eckman, Lester. *The History of the Musar Movement 1840–1945*. New York: Shengold Publishers, Inc., 1975.

Elias, Joseph. "Israel Salanter." In *Jewish Leaders 1750–1940*, edited by Leo Jung. Jerusalem: Boys Town Jerusalem Press, 1964.

Epstein, Joseph D. "Yeshivat Mir." In *Mosdot Torah B'Ayropah B'Vinyanam Uv'hurbanam*, edited by Samuel K. Mirsky, 87–132. New York: Histadruth Ha'Ivrit B'America, 1956.

Ever, Isaac. *Harav Yehuda Herschel Levenberg: Zein Leben und Kampf*. Cleveland: Ivry, 1939.

Gat, B.Z. *Ha-Yishuv ha-Yehudi B'Eretz Yisrael*. Jerusalem, 1962.

Glitzenstein, Abraham H. *Tomche T'mimim*. New York: United Yeshivot Tomchei T'mimim Lubavitch, 1969.

Glenn, Menahem G. *Israel Salanter, Religious Ethical Thinker: The Story of a Religious Ethical Current in 19th Century Judaism*. Published for the Dropsie College for Hebrew and Cognate Learning. New York: Bloch, 1953.

Gross, Alexander, and Kaminetsky, Joseph. "Shraga Feivel Mendlovitz." In *Men of the Spirit*, edited by Leo Jung. New York: Bloch,-1964.

Hakohen, Israel Meir. *Mishnah Berurah*. Jerusalem: Monzon, 1946.

———. *Sefer Shmirat Halashon*. Jerusalem: Vaad Sh'mirat Halashon, 1967.

———. *Minhat Yehudah V'Yerushalayim*. Union City, N.J.: Yisroel Sovo Institute, 1979.

Helmreich, William B. *The World of the Yeshiva: An Intimate Portrait of Orthodox Jewry*. New York: Free Press, 1982.

Hoel, Paul G. *Introduction to Mathematical Statistics*. New York: John Wiley and Sons, 1966.

Horowitz, Zvi Halevi Ish. *Letoldot Hakehilot B'Polin*. Jerusalem: Mossad Harav Kook, 1978.

Jacobs, Louis. *Hasidic Thought*. New York: Behrman House, 1976.

Katz, Dov. *The Musar Movement, Its History, Leading Personalities and Doctrines*. Translated by Leonard Oschrey. Tel Aviv: Orly Press, 1977.

Klaperman, Gilbert. *The Story of Yeshiva University*. New York: Macmillan, 1969.

Kranzler, David. *Japanese, Nazis and Jews: The Jewish Refugee Community of Shanghai, 1938–1945*. New York: Yeshiva University, 1976.

Levovitz, Simcha Zizel. *Hokhmah Umusar*. New York: Aber Press, 1957.

Margolis, Isidor. *Jewish Teacher Training Schools in the United States*. New York: Mizrachi-Hapoel Hamizrachi, 1964.

Mirsky, Samuel K., ed. *Mosdot Torah B'Ayropah Bevinyanam Uv'hurbanam*. New York: Histadruth Ha'Ivrit B'America, 1956.

Pakudah, Bahya ibn. *Hovot Halevavot*. Jerusalem: Boys Town Jerusalem Press, 1962.

Rosen, Kopul. *Rabbi Israel Salanter and the Musar Movement*. London, 1943.

Rothkoff, Aaron. *Bernard Revel: Builder of American Jewish Orthodoxy.* Philadelphia: Jewish Publication Society, 1972.

Schiff, Alvin I. *The Jewish Day School in America.* New York: Jewish Education Committee Press, 1966.

Seidman, Hillel. *Shraga Feivel Mendlowitz.* New York: Shengold Publishers, Inc., 1976.

————. "Yeshivat Ez Hayyim D'Klezk." In *Mosdot Torah B'Ayropah B'vinyanam Uv'hurbanam*, edited by S.K. Mirsky, 239–42. New York: Histadruth Ha'Ivrit B'America, 1956.

————. "Yeshivat Lubavitch." In *Mosdot Torah B'Ayropah B'vinyanam Uv'hurbanam*, edited by Samuel K. Mirsky, 337–53. New York: Histadruth Ha'Ivrit B'America, 1956.

Solomon, M. *Three Generations in the Yishuv.* (Hebrew). Jerusalem, 5702.

Tauber, Azriel, ed. *Yisaschar B'Ohalekhah.* Monsey, N.Y.: Mechon Hahoyroa, 1979.

Wolfson, Harry Austryn. *Crescas' Critique of Aristotle.* Cambridge: Harvard University Press, 1929.

Yacow, Rabbi Nahum. *The History of the Mir Yeshivah in America.* New York: Mir Yeshiva Central Institute, 1978.

Yosher, Moses M. "Israel Meir HaKohen, the Hafetz Hayyim." In *Jewish Leaders*, edited by Leo Jung. Jerusalem: Boys Town Jerusalem Press, 1974.

Articles

Bakst, Nechama. "Woman at the Crossroads." *The Jewish Observer* (February 1982): 14–16.

Berkovitz, Eliezer. "A Contemporary Rabbinical School for Orthodox Jewry." *Tradition* (Fall 1971): 5–21.

Egozi, Akiba. "Beit Medrash Govoha beLakewood." *Sheviley Hahinukh* (Winter 1962).

Feinstein, R. Moshe. "The Partnership of Yissachar and Zebulun." *Am HaTorah* 5 (1982): 5–31.

Jacobson, B. "Torah Returns to Its Lodging." *Zanz* (14 May 1982): 3.

Kaminetsky, Yaakov. "Filling the Void: Reflection on the Passing of a Godol." *The Jewish Observer* (October 1976): 15–19.

Kaplan, Aryeh. "A Get in Monsey." *The Jewish Observer* (December 1976): 15–19.

————. "Variations on the Yissachar-Zevulun Theme." *The Jewish Observer* (January 1978): 23–26.

Kranzler, Gershon. "Challenge and Commitment." *The Jewish Observer* (April 1978): 3–6.

Menahem, Y. "Der Bais Din Fun Kolel Mechon L'horaya in Monsey." *Dos Yiddishe Vort* (Iyar–Sivan 1983): 42.

Perr, Yechiel J. "The Yeshiva World and Orthodoxy: Self-Protection or Encounter." *The Jewish Observer* (January 1970): 22–23.

Rokeach, Mendel. "The Kolel: American Phase." *Jewish Life* (May–June 1967): 13–21.

Singer, David. "The Yeshivah World." *Commentary* (October 1976): 70–73.

Spivak, Yaacov. "The Kollel Horabonim: Torah Answers to Explosive Questions." *The World Jewish Tribune,* 18 January 1980, 8–10.

————. "The Jewish Divorce and Those Who 'Forget' to Get a Get." *The World Jewish Tribune*, 7 March 1980, 11-12.

Wolbe, Shlomo. "The Yeshiva Today: The Significance of this Institution Throughout Our History and in Our Days." *The Jewish Observer* (April, 1970): 8–10.

————. "Higher Horizons Down Under: An Australian Torah Connection." *The Jewish Observer* (November 1981): 26–28.

Wolpin, Nisson. "The Community Kolel: Reaching Out With Torah." *The Jewish Observer* (October 1979); 19–26.

School Publications

Alumni Newsletter. Beth Medrash Govoha, New Jersey: March 1981.
Bulletin. Undergraduate Division. Beth Medrash Govoha of Lakewood, New Jersey: 1977.
"Excerpts from Recent Remarks of Rabbi Chaim Fasman Regarding Aims, Activities and Achievement." Kollel Bais Avrohom of Los Angeles. Mimeo. n.d.
Kollel Bais Avrohom Newsletter. September–October 1981; November–December 1981.
Kuntres Or HaKolel. Baltimore: Ner Israel, 1980.
Ner Israel Rabbinical College Bulletin. Baltimore: Ner Israel, 1982.
Purpose. New York: Yeshiva Chaim Berlin, n.d.
Tenth Anniversary Souvenir Journal. New York: Yeshiva Chaim Berlin, 1966.
The Lubavitcher Rebbe. New York: Merkos L'inyonei Chinuch, 1978.

Self-Studies

Abbreviation: AARTS = Association of Advanced Rabbinical and Talmudic Schools

Central Yeshiva Tomchei Tmimim-Lubavitch, Catalogue 1979–80. New York: Chabad-Lubavitch, 1980.
Central Yeshiva Tomchei Tmimim: Self-Study. New York: AARTS, 1976.
Mir Yeshiva Central Institute: Self-Study. New York: AARTS, 1975.
Yeshiva Chaim Berlin: Self-Study. New York: AARTS, 1975.
Yeshiva Eitz Chaim of Bobov: Self-Study. New York: AARTS, 1975.
Yeshiva Ner Israel: Self-Study. New York: AARTS, 1981.
Yeshivat Rabbi Israel Meir HaKohen: Self-Study. New York: AARTS, 1975.

Unpublished Works

Blass, Thomas. Social Structure and Social Organization in a Rabbinical Seminary. Papers written for Prof. J. Gumperz at Bernard Revel Graduate School, Yeshiva University, January 1967.
Feuerman, Chaim. "A Study of Views of the Principal's Role in Elementary Orthodox Hebrew Day Schools in the New York City Area: Expectations Held by Principals and Their Lay Board Chairman." Ph. D. diss., St John's University, 1977.
Greenwald, Eli B. "Rabbinic Education in the United States: 1867–1939." Ph. D. diss., Dropsie University, 1975.
Lewitter, Sidney Rubin. "A School for Scholars, the Beth Medrash Govoha, The Rabbi Aaron Kotler Jewish Institute of Higher Learning in Lakewood, New Jersey." Ed.D. diss., Rutgers University, 1981.
Lieberman, Sidney. "A Historical Study of the Development of the Yeshiva High School Curriculum." Ph. D. diss., Yeshiva University, 1959.

Interviews

Adlerstein, R. Jeffrey. Alumnus of Kolel Ner David. January 1982.
Bendheim, Charles. Board member of RIETS. March 1982.
Borny, Chaim. Kolel fellow. August 1983.
Cyperstein, Seymour. Son of the first *Rosh Hakolel* at Yeshiva University. March 1982.
Fasman, R. Chaim. Founder and dean of Kollel Bais Avrohom of Los Angeles. January 1982.
Feifer, Hayyim, and Feifer, Moses. Rabbis who had studied in Kletsk and Shanghai. February 1982.

Fink, Dov. *Kolel* fellow in Gur Aryeh. April 1982.

Fisher, R. Eliyahu. *Rosh Hakolel* of Gur. June 1982.

Gibber, Robert. Executive Director of Yeshiva Zichron Moshe. July and August 1983.

Ginzburg, R. Eliezer. Faculty member in Mirrer Kolel, formerly in charge of *haburah* assignments. April 1983.

Glazer, Samuel. Executive Director of the Ner Israel Kolel. May 1982.

Goldberger, R. Yonassen. *Rosh Hakolel* of Kolel Avreikhim of Bobov. May 1982.

Gorelick, R. Abba. Dean of Kolel Zichron Moshe. July 1983.

Halberstam, R. Jekuthiel Judah. Klausenberger *Rebbe*. June 1982.

Handelsman, R. Moses. Executive Director of the Mir Yeshiva. October 1981.

Heller, R. Joseph I. *Rosh Hakolel* of Chabad-Lubavitch. January 1982.

Hodakov, R.M.A. Treasurer of Machne Israel, the Chabad Social Welfare Organization. March 1982.

Kahn, R. Aharon. *Rosh Hakolel* of the Kolel Elyon at Yeshiva University. March 1983.

Kalmanowitz, R. Shrage Moshe. *Rosh Yeshivah* of Mirrer Yeshiva Central Institute. September–October 1981.

Klor, Noach. *Kolel* fellow at Beth Medrash Govoha. January 1982.

Kotlarsky, R. Moshe. Director of Development of Chabad Houses. December 1981.

Kotler, R. Shneur. *Rosh Yeshivah* of Beth Medrash Govoha, Lakewood, N.J. January 1982.

Krone, Moshe. Director of the Torah Culture Department of the Jewish Agency. August 1981.

Kuperman, R. Eliezer. Director of Student Relations at Beth Medrash Govoha. January 1982.

Lamm, R. Norman. President of Yeshiva University. March 1982.

Landesman, R. Leib. Dean of Kollel Horabonim. June 1982.

Leibowitz, R. Henoch. *Rosh Yeshivah* of Kolel Ner David of Yeshivat Rabbi Israel Meir HaKohen. March 1982.

Lieff, R. David. Past President of the Rabbinical Board of Flatbush. November 1981.

Lesser, R. Dov. Torah Umesorah, the National Association of Hebrew Day Schools. December 1981.

Levovitz, R. Pesach. Congregational spiritual leader in Lakewood, N.J. June 1982.

Mashinsky, Yankel. Senior *kolel* fellow, Zanz. June 1982.

Mayer, R. Shmuel. Alumnus of Kolel Beth Medrash Govoha.

Miller, R. Israel. Senior Vice President at Yeshiva University. June 1982.

Rosenfeld, Mendel. *Kolel* student of Kolel Avreichim of Lubavitch. January 1982.

Ruderman, R. Jacob. *Rosh Yeshivah* at Yeshiva Ner Israel of Baltimore. April 1982.

Schachter, R. Herschel. *Rosh Hakolel* at the Marcos and Adina Katz Kolel at Yeshiva University. May 1982.

Schechter, R. Aaron. *Rosh Yeshivah* at Yeshiva Chaim Berlin. April 1982.

Schoenblum, Moshe. *Kolel* fellow at Mir. January 1982.

Schmidman, R. Morris. Executive Director of the Boro Park Council of Jewish Organizations. June 1982.

Tauber, R. Azriel. President of Kolel Mechon Hahoyroa. June 1982.

Tauber, R. Eliezer, *Rosh Hakolel* of Kolel Mechoin Hahoyroa. June 1982.

Tropper, R. Daniel. *Mashgi'ah* of Kolel Ner David. November 1981.

Weiderman, Bezalal. *Kolel* fellow in Kolel Zichron Moshe. 17 August 1983.

Weiner, R. Yakov T. Director of the *Mekhinah* of Mechon Hahoyroa. June 1982.

Wolman, Shmuel. Director of the Gur Aryeh Kolel. April 1982.

Index